Triangulating Religion, Belief, *and* Faith
in the Twenty-First Century

Triangulating Religion, Belief, *and* Faith *in the* Twenty-First Century

Theological Briefs

BRADFORD McCALL

WIPF & STOCK · Eugene, Oregon

TRIANGULATING RELIGION, BELIEF, AND FAITH IN THE TWENTY-FIRST CENTURY
Theological Briefs

Wipf & Stock
An Imprint of Wipf and Stock Publishers
199 W. 8th Ave., Suite 3
Eugene, OR 97401

www.wipfandstock.com

PAPERBACK ISBN: 979-8-3852-2789-1
HARDCOVER ISBN: 979-8-3852-2790-7
EBOOK ISBN: 979-8-3852-2791-4

VERSION NUMBER 01/09/25

Contents

Dedication

I AM THE AGE now that I am experiencing more and more of the older people in my life passing away. Especially has this been true lately with respect to those individuals who had great impact on my early life. Even more specific, this has been especially true regarding a couple of church teachers from my early years of life to whom I dedicate this book. For example, Mrs. Bonnie Dortch taught me in Vacation Bible School for several years at the local First Baptist Church in Hawkinsville, Georgia. She was a lovely lady in all manners of that terminology. To be honest, I have not only loved her eldest daughter Jamie for what seems like millennia, but I also adored her as well. Mrs. Bonnie was a faith-full woman, and those early years of Vacation Bible School teaching have, subconsciously, been one of the reasons that I have—at a later time—come back to the *religion*, *belief*, and *faith* of my youth. Although I no longer adhere to a Southern Baptist form of the faith, the *essentials* of *religion*, *belief*, and *faith* were instilled in me from an early age, particularly from Mrs. Bonnie Dortch and other spirited people at First Baptist Church. Mrs. Bonnie was taken too soon from among us. I dedicate this book to her.

That said, I would also like to dedicate this book to a second individual who also impacted my spiritual life and physical life greatly at First Baptist, Hawkinsville: Larry Gattis, MD. Dr. Gattis was my Sunday School teacher for several years in my early teens. Dr. Gattis not only was a lively teacher, but he also invested much time and resources in activities for us young teenagers who were fortunate enough to be associated with him. Whether it was weekend bowling trips, or time spent at his pool house, or even weeklong camping trips to nearby mountains, Dr. Gattis was a great youth leader. I stated earlier that I greatly appreciate his role in my spiritual *and* physical life. Dr. Gattis was one of the first people on the scene of my horrific September 6, 1995, vehicular accident, and he was mainly responsible therefore for the continuance of my life thereafter. From 1995 through 2022 when he passed away, I regularly saw him when I made a trip to my hometown. He knew my physical and mental limitations and "other problems" better than any specialist doctor could, due in no small part to his care for me as a person *before* his care for me as a patient. He not only was the main reason I survived the traumatic brain injury in 1995 due to his primary care on the scene of the accident, but he also continued to bring me back from the depth of despair for smaller issues several times thereafter as well. Alike unto Mrs. Bonnie spoken of above, Dr. Gattis was no doubt instrumental in my eventual coming back to the *religion, belief,* and *faith* of my youth after college.

The world is less rich now with both of them gone from among us.

About the Author

DR. BRADFORD L. McCALL holds a BS in biology (2000), four master's degrees in religion or philosophy (2005, MDiv from Asbury Theological Seminary; 2011, MA in church history and doctrine from Regent University; 2017, MA in systematic philosophy from Holy Apostles College and Seminary; 2020, MA in religious studies from Claremont School of Theology), and a PhD in comparative theology from Claremont School of Theology in Claremont, California, wherein his dissertation was entitled "Contingency and Divine Activity: Toward a Contemporary Conception of Divine Involvement in an Evolutionary World," which was successfully defended September 22, 2021. His *Doktorvater* and dissertation chair was the distinguished Dr. Philip Clayton. The other members of his committee were similarly distinguished in their areas of expertise: Dr. Ingolf U. Dalferth and Dr. Roland Faber. In addition to the present book, McCall has written or is in the process of writing nearly a dozen books: *A Modern Relation of Theology and Science Assisted by Emergence and Kenosis* (Eugene, OR: Wipf & Stock, 2018); *Evolution: Secular or Sacred?* (Eugene, OR: Wipf & Stock, 2020); *The God of Chance and Purpose: Divine Involvement in a Secular Evolutionary World* (Eugene, OR: Wipf & Stock, 2022); *Macroevolution, Contingency and Divine Activity: Divine Involvement Through*

About the Author

Uncontrolling, Amorepotent Love in an Evolutionary World (Eugene, OR: Pickwick, 2023); as editor, *Reading Ruse: Michael Ruse on Darwinism, Science, and Faith,* with an autobiographical chapter by Michael Ruse (Eugene, OR: Cascade, 2024); and as editor, *Ruminating on Ruse: Key Themes in the Evolutionary Naturalism of Michael Ruse* (Eugene, OR: Cascade, forthcoming).

1

Toward Faith Alone as the Ultimate Concern

Introduction

I ADMIT IT UP front: this book is a combination of various independently produced articles I have written over the last five years that are broadly related to one another. They are unpublished heretofore. That said, they are related to each other in that they are all concerned with faith, belief, and religion in general, and comparative theology explicitly. These chapters were part of the foundation for my comprehensive exams pursuant to a PhD in comparative theology at Claremont School of Theology in Claremont, California, during the summer of 2020. I was granted said PhD in May 2022 from Claremont School of Theology, and since that time I have been working on a rewrite of my dissertation and putting out various other fires. While one could argue that these various chapters do not cling together tightly, I posit that when read together, they will give one the ability to make new inroads to understanding how faith, belief, and religion not only differ but also how they can contribute to comparative theology. The three topics broadly covered herein can heighten the understanding of the sacred by those who study them.

Toward Faith Alone as the Ultimate Concern

While one could write numerous dissertation-length manuscripts on these three topics, the general concern of this new series entitled "Theological Briefs" is to be just that: brief. However, this does not mean that serious academic reflection has been excised from these pages that follow. Rather, each book within this new series is calculated to be "bare bones" as much as possible without doing violence to the topic at hand. This means that ordinary filler words and filler material will be eclipsed in this series. We aim to present the reader with a short, concise, and potent introduction to material under review within the parameters of 125 to 150 pages, or, that is, somewhere between 30,000 to 35,000 words in toto. We believe that this can be done across the broad range of theological topics if the authors consciously restrain themselves in their expository endeavors.

As to a few preliminaries, what is *faith*? Further, what is *belief*? Which one comes first in a person's journey toward the sacred? Moreover, does *religion* factor into these two terms, and, if so, where and how? Does Augustine's well-worn line "faith seeking understanding" mean anything today? If it does, would it mean belief comes prior to faith and/or religion? One can argue both sides of this debate and still be considered "orthodox," seemingly. Perhaps it is the case that belief precedes faith most of the time, but not all of the time (?). Perhaps it is the other way around. A further question is what, exactly, is the demarcation between belief and faith? Many a person believes a thing to be true in their very bones; it would seem to me that such a stance borders on what is commonly referred to as faith. Is religion the combination of belief and faith together into a coherent system of thought, or is it emergent from the two, existing as a separate mental (or spiritual) entity?

We will begin our approach within this book by exploring methods and perspectives in comparative religion, which amounts to a body of methods, rules, and postulates employed by a discipline or a person—that is, a particular procedure or set of procedures. I will explore the approaches of four major comparative religious theorists, including their perceived strengths, limitations, and any possible interconnections between them. Indeed, in chapter 2 I will examine the theology of Paul F. Knitter—a Roman Catholic—as being global. Then, in chapter 3, I will investigate Robert Cummings Neville, who is a United Methodist and an admirer of process thought. We shall be aided in our journey to understand comparative approaches methodologically thereby. The next chapter, the fourth, will likewise pursue the methodological similarities and differences between the foregoing thinkers and David Ray Griffin, who is a member of the United Church of Christ and is a full-fledged process theologian. Chapter 5 scrutinizes Roland Faber, who is an adherent to the Bahá'í faith and also a highly regarded process thinker in his own right.

The four chapters of part 2 all concern Paul Tillich or Wilfred Cantwell Smith in one way or another. Indeed, chapter 6 begins part 2 and shifts from methodology to praxis by analyzing two great thinkers with respect to faith, belief, and religion, starting off with Wilfred Cantwell Smith, and then analyzing Paul Tillich regarding the same. Chapter 7 explores Tillich and Smith on belief and faith in particular. The eighth chapter scrutinizes the key to all things, wherein Tillich and Smith offer their thoughts on faith alone. The final chapter—number 9—will close the volume in its entirety with a hearty conclusion and some prospects for further research. Within it, I proffer a particularly nuanced Tillichian conclusion.

The Multitude of Religions

Why are there so many religions? If God is one, should not all religion(s) in fact be one? Are all religions, given the plurality, valid in God's eyes—equally placing people in front of the divine source of all life? Are their differences more a matter of the flavor of the expression, rather than truly conflicting content? In the early 1960s, Wilfred Cantwell Smith inspired many "pluralists-to-be" with the resolve to search for a theology of religious pluralism with the following statement, one which has only grown more relevant in the years that have passed since then. Indeed, Smith states,

> The religious life of mankind, from now on, if it is to be
> lived at all, will be lived in the context of religious plural-
> ism. This is true for all of us. . . . No longer are people

of other persuasions peripheral or distant. . . . The more
alert we are, . . . the more we are finding that they are our
neighbors, our colleagues, our competitors, our fellows.
. . . Increasingly, not only is our civilization's destiny af-
fected by their actions; but we drink coffee with them
personally as well.[1]

Smith also noted, in the same volume, the following, which
rightly serves for me as a prolegomenon for the entire book you
have begun to read:

How does one account, theologically, for the fact of [hu-
manity's] religious diversity? This is really as big an issue,
almost, as the question of how one accounts theologically for evil—but Christian theologians have been much
more conscious of the fact of evil than that of religious
pluralism. . . . From now on any serious intellectual statement of the Christian faith must include, if it is to serve
its purpose, . . . some sort of doctrine of other religions.[2]

For Smith, within the pattern(s) of faith, there is a meaning—
a deep and intangible significance that is symbolized; beyond the
forms there is substance—or the intimation of a transcending, lim-
itless truth. This infinite becomes in part available to us within the
finite, through these finite channels that a society inherits and cher-
ishes and uses to express its faith and to nourish it. Can we learn
something of that faith, and appreciate in part that inner meaning,
by exploring the significance of these outward forms? This is the
task of comparative religion: not only to ascertain the institutions,
beliefs, and practices of a tradition but to ascertain also what these
things mean to those who participate in them. Religious truth (plural) lies not in symbols but in what is symbolized—if only we can
apprehend it.[3] A qualification, however, flows from this: of course
we cannot apprehend it fully; not only can the outsider never grasp
in its entirety what a tradition means to those within it, but even
those within never apprehend fully. This is altogether proper, since

1. Smith, *Faith of Other Men*, 11.
2. Smith, *Faith of Other Men*, 132–33.
3. Smith, *Patterns of Faith*, 52.

religious symbols symbolize the infinite, or at the very least symbolize what is greater than we. The whole point of any religious tradition, after all, lies in the fact that it introduces us to what is greater than we and greater than itself.[4]

Among the various schools of philosophy within contemporary Western culture, one proposes a vision of reality that is inherently agreeable with what most people experience in their everyday lives: that the world and everything in it are evolutionary, or in process. We are, then, not in a static state, but in a state of *becoming*. Alfred North Whitehead and Charles Hartshorne see this world, correctly in my opinion, as a world that is entangled with creativity in and through process. Chapter 4 will attempt to, however minutely, make these implications of Whitehead's and Hartshorne's philosophy more overt.

Now, as I begin my journey into multi-religious methodology and meanings, let me start with Knitter. I do so for a couple of reasons: he was—by far!—the easiest to understand and amalgamate; also, however, he is the least "process-y" of all the names to be covered. In fact, one can perceive in my order choice an increasing focus on process philosophical themes in the authors to be examined, covered, and synthesized. It is only fitting, then, that I end with Roland Faber because I perceive him to be the most process-based scholar among the four. With that said, let me step into Knitter.

---

4. Smith, *Patterns of Faith*, 52–53.

PART I

Four Comparative
Religious Theorists

2

Paul F. Knitter

A World Theologian

Paul Knitter is the Paul Tillich Professor Emeritus of Theology, World Religions and Culture at Union Theological Seminary in New York and a leading theologian of religious pluralism. Knitter holds a licentiate in theology from the Pontifical Gregorian University in Rome and a doctorate from the University of Marburg, Germany, the first of which is particularly also poignant to me. Since his 1985 book *No Other Name? A Critical Survey of Christian Attitudes Toward the World Religions*,[1] Knitter has been exploring religious pluralism and interreligious dialogue. One would think that since that is where Knitter "starts," I would begin my examination of him there too; but I contend that several of his later books tell the story of Knitter's methodology, meanings, and implications far better.

Indeed, I shall begin this examination of Knitter with his 2005 edition of *Introducing Theologies of Religions* in part because it is the most comprehensive coverage of his own views, and because it reflects his mature thought. I will then proceed through *The Myth of Religious Superiority*, and then move backward in a sense to its

---

1. Please see the bibliography for information about sources cited in the text.

precursor volume, *The Myth of Christian Uniqueness*. I will then reflect upon Knitter and Haight's *Jesus and Buddha: Friends in Conversation*, only to then reflect upon Knitter's personal multi-faith journey as recounted in *Without Buddha I Could Not Be a Christian*. All the while, I shall incorporate insights into Knitter received from Leonard Swidler and Paul Mojzes's *The Uniqueness of Jesus: A Dialogue with Paul F. Knitter*, along with a few insights from Robert B. Stewart's *Can Only One Religion Be True? Paul Knitter and Harold Netland in Dialogue*.

Knitter starts his *Introducing Theologies of Religions* with a comment that in our present age, one needs to be "religiously inter-religious," in part because "to walk one's own faith-path, one needs to be walking with others from different paths."[2] The entirety of *Introducing Theologies of Religions* attempts to do just that: explain how and why one needs to be at least aware, if not conversant, of others' faith(s). Knitter notes that previous generations—almost to the one—have not had to face this type of situation in which we find ourselves today. These sorts of questions lead Knitter to ask, more specifically, "how should *my* religion relate to the others?"[3] Might he (and we) not learn more from other religions than we have from our own?

For Knitter, the theology of religions, or as now oft stated, the theology of religious pluralism, wrestles with such questions and issues. Knitter contends that there has been growth in the sentimentality of religious pluralism that needs to be taken into account of because of our changed "historical circumstances."[4] What the Jew once could say about the Muslim, or the Christian the Jew, is no longer adequate. One cannot dismiss forthrightly and summarily the claims made by other religions, perhaps most of all because one cannot deny the grace, love, and truth exhibited by other religions. For Knitter, this last implication applies as much to Muslims as for Jews, as for Buddhists, as for Hindus, as for Confucians, and as for Christians. After all, in today's world, the reality of other religions

---

2. Knitter, *Introducing Theologies of Religions*, xi.

3. Knitter, *Introducing Theologies of Religions*, 1 (emphasis added).

4. Knitter, *Introducing Theologies of Religions*, 3.

no longer exists across the border; it has moved to our very neighborhoods, throughout the entire world, but nowhere more strikingly than in North America and Europe.[5]

For Knitter, we do not, first of all, exist and only then relate; rather, it is our relating that serves as the foundation of *what* we do, *how* we do it, and *with* whom or *what* we do it. For him, the "many are called to be one."[6] But this one does *not* devour the many. In effect, he notes, that there is a "unitive pluralism" or a "plurality constituting unity."[7] In effect, then, there is a movement underway toward a truly dialogical community, one in which each member lives through dialogue with others. Thus, as Knitter advocated, one must be religious interreligiously in today's world.

Knitter, in his *Introducing Theologies of Religions*,[8] points out that there are, widely, four main options when it comes to religious pluralism: the Replacement model; the Fulfillment model; the Mutuality model; and the Acceptance model. These four models move from the most restrictive to the least restrictive. Indeed, the Replacement model, according to Knitter, teaches that there is, in the final analysis, only one true religion, and that is far too often considered to be nothing else than Christianity. This model held sway throughout the majority of history, and still has very vociferous representatives from fundamentalists, both (Neo-) and Evangelicals, along with various charismatics. In this view, God's religion is the true religion, and it is Christianity. This "theology of total replacement," so to speak, looks at other faith communities as so lacking, so aberrant, that sometime before the end—or at the end!—Christianity will move in and take their place(s). For most of the twentieth century, Karl Barth was this view's most nimble and able advocate. Although Barth himself was no fundamentalist,

---

5. Lightly adapted from Knitter, *Introducing Theologies of Religions*, 1–17.

6. Knitter, *Introducing Theologies of Religions*, 10.

7. Knitter, *Introducing Theologies of Religions*, 10.

8. Chapters 1–5 of this text cover sequentially these models, the first two of which I am very familiar with, for that—evangelicalism—is from which I was bred. The "breakthrough" occurred, at least for the Catholic church, at Vatican II, I am becoming increasingly aware of, since that is the church to which I now belong, and have studied at the graduate level.

he nevertheless laid the proverbial foundation for fundamentalist thought through Replacement model thinking, mostly by asserting that *the* Bible is the one and only word of God, and therefore the only view with which to perceive other religions.

Notably, even the "New Evangelicals," the chastised believers of old fundamentalism mostly, are people firmly committed to the uniqueness of Jesus, but are—largely—at the same time more open, more amenable, and more charitable than the ultra-conservative, (Neo-)Evangelicals and the various charismatic groups. They affirm that revelation exists in other religions, but on the point of whether there can be "salvation" per se outside of Jesus of Nazareth (the "Christ"), they are on the same footing as the (Neo-)Evangelicals: in no way is this possible. These "New Evangelicals," though, do accede that other religions can be preparation for the gospel of Jesus.[9] For this reason, the "New Evangelicals" serve as a bridge of sorts from the Replacement model to the Fulfillment model, to which we now turn.

The Fulfillment model,[10] as described by Knitter, contends that the one fulfills the many. This is highlighted in the *weak* pluralist ontology of the Second Vatican Council, for example; this model asserts that the love of God is universal, but also that God's love is particular: that is, it is made real in Jesus of Nazareth. The Fulfillment model balances this "dance" in a much different way than does the Replacement model. If the Replacement model was the majority opinion throughout Christian history, it is safe to say that the Fulfillment model has, from the second half of the twentieth century until today, *replaced it*. Indeed, the Fulfillment model characterizes the stance of the "mainline" churches, comprised of Lutheran, Anglican, Methodist, and my own Roman Catholic Church. These churches, largely, contend that other religions are of value, that God is to be found in them, and that Christians need to be open to dialogue with them, not simply pursue converting them. Notably, Karl Rahner is the pioneer of this approach, especially within the confines of the Catholic Church; the very centerpiece of Rahner's

9. Knitter, *Introducing Theologies of Religions*, 19–60.

10. Knitter, *Introducing Theologies of Religions*, 63–99.

theology is that *God is love*, which has ramifications, for him, to dialogue with other religions. Indeed, in *Foundations of Christian Faith*, Rahner even made an assertion that was quite startling at the time: God's grace is active in other religions insomuch as God is offering himself in and through other religious practices, beliefs, and rituals.[11] From his conclusion that Jesus is the reason why God pours out love to all of the natural world, Rahner further concludes that people of other religious persuasions, too, have love poured out to them. In fact, any Buddhist, Hindu, or non-Christian who experiences God's love, is *already* connected to the divine through Jesus, for Jesus is the pinnacle of God's gift of love; they are, in a sense, already Christians—*anonymous* Christians, in his wording. In no small way, Rahner's writings provided an, if not the, impetus for modern religious pluralism insomuch as he directly impacted the Vatican II Council, and his reach also extended to various mainline Protestant denominations.

The third model used by Knitter, i.e., the Mutuality model, is summed up in the statement that there are many true religions called to dialogue. Here three bridges have been used by Christians to relate to those on different paths: the philosophical-historical bridge, the religious-mystical bridge, and the ethical-practical bridge. Marcus Borg is a prominent advocate of this view. He writes, "I am convinced that there are millions of mainline Christians . . . for whom the statement that Christianity is not the only true religion is 'good news.' . . . We are living in a time when many Christians are beginning to let go of exclusivist [read Replacement model] and absolutist [read Fulfillment model] claims."[12] If the Fulfillment model placed more heavy emphasis on Jesus' particularity, this Mutuality model places the emphasis upon God's universal love and his presence in other religions.[13] This Mutuality model asks, largely, How can Christians engage in a more fulfilling and authentic dialogue with persons of other faith groups; further, How can we create a playing field that is level, so to speak, for the dialogue to occur; and, How can we come

11. Rahner, *Foundations of Christian Faith*, 178–203.
12. Borg, "Jesus and Buddhism," 96.
13. Knitter, *Introducing Theologies of Religions*, 109.

Part I: Four Comparative Religious Theorists

to a clearer understanding of Jesus' uniqueness (if any) that will sustain the dialogue? These Mutualists seek to combine elements that do not easily go together, for they want to preserve the real diversity and differences inherent in world religions, *but* . . . they seek something in common betwixt the various religions that makes the game of dialogue possible in the first place.[14] These types of Christians understand that one cannot go into a dialogue insisting that Jesus is the *only* way, the *only* truth, and the *only* life. If they did, no dialogue would be possible at all, for Jesus would simply win in the end. They seek true dialogue wherein each participant can learn as much as possible from the religious "other." Mysticism is oft seen to be an effective bridge to use within this Mutuality model, for the divine is appreciated to be ineffable, i.e., more than anyone experiences in one particular religion.

Raimon Panikkar is a representative of the mysticism side of this Mutuality model; notably, he insists upon the "mutual fecundation" amid variously different religious communities. By relating to each other in mutual fecundation, various groups of religious communities will all discover and expand their own identities, not simply be "exposed" to other religions. John Hick is an able representative of this Mutuality model as well, as verified in his 1973 writing that religion/theology needs to undergo a Copernican-like revolution "in our conception of the universe of other faiths and the place of our own religion within it . . . [which demands] a paradigm shift from a Christianity-centered or Jesus-centered to a God-centered model of the universe of faiths. One then sees the great world religions as different human responses to the one divine Reality."[15] Overall, this Mutuality model pictures Jesus as a sacrament of God's love rather than a satisfaction for God's justice, and focuses upon a Spirit-Christology rather than a Logos-Christology.[16]

The Acceptance model of Knitter embraces a (radical?) form of inclusivism. It recognizes that real differences make for real dialogue and one of the best ways to understand one's own religion

14. Knitter, *Introducing Theologies of Religions*, 111.
15. Hick, *God and the Universe of Faiths*, 131.
16. Knitter, *Introducing Theologies of Religions*, 150–51.

14

is through comparing it to others. This last model is appealing to me since it gives free rein to the Spirit who is always blowing in the wind. Or, as I put it elsewhere, we are never able to wrap our mind around what the Spirit is up to. This approach to other faiths seems to think that it is better, as a proverbial child of the times, to speak of the way people actually understand themselves, today! This model is heavily correlated with the full acceptance of a postmodern mindset, for postmodernists may not know what they are seeking per se, but they definitely know what they are not seeking. So then, in a sense, this approach is apophatic.

As full-fledged postmodernists, these Acceptance model thinkers corporately distrust all claims to universal truth (i.e., metanarratives), decry the denial of mystical views of the world, abhor the primary usage of empirical data, and are leery of an excessive confidence in the power of reason.[17] According to Knitter, this Acceptance model, fundamentally, is based upon postliberal foundations, founded on the notion that many religions means there are many *salvations*, and it calls us to the direly critical exploration of comparative theology, whereby people put aside their misgivings about other religions, and simply take a deep dive into the study and embrace of another religion.[18] George Lindbeck, who notes that there is "no common ground" among many religions and that is, so to say, "OK,"[19] would be a great representative of this view along with S. Mark Heim, who characteristically remarks that "Nirvana and communion with God are contradictory only if we assume that one or the other must be the sole fate for all human beings."[20] Though not stated explicitly by him, I think that Knitter's sentiments also lie with this group, i.e., the Acceptance model.

Knitter's *The Myth of Religious Superiority: A Multifaith Exploration* is a sequel to his and John Hick's *The Myth of Christian Uniqueness: Toward a Pluralistic Theology of Religions*. I cover the second volume first, and the first volume second, in what follows.

17. Knitter, *Introducing Theologies of Religions*, 174–75.

18. Knitter, *Introducing Theologies of Religions*, 177.

19. Lindbeck, *Nature of Doctrine*, 49.

20. Heim, *Salvations: Truth and Difference in Religions*, 149.

Knitter notes at the onset of the second volume that religious language bears the quality of the mythic, symbolic, metaphoric, and the poetic types of writings. Religion's truth, then, depends innately upon interpretation, which will necessarily be different in different cultures and in different eras.[21] Knitter herein asserts that claims to superiority can ipso facto, at the most, only ground competition; they cannot promote cooperation and mutual learning.[22] As such, they can allow *tolerance*, but not mutuality (remember my earlier assertion that I think Knitter is an advocate of the Acceptance model of religious pluralism). Knitter, at the onset of this title, notes the quasi-conclusions of the conference from which this title sprang. He lists six in number, which I will below delineate in brief fashion, starting from the most bold to the least:[23]

1. All religions contain the resources, *within* their very selves, to adopt the pluralist model. The pluralist turn, thus, is not an imposition, but rather the gradual outworking of resources with which every faith is endowed. Religious pluralists, then, should think themselves to be faithful to their own religious communities of membership;

2. Differences between religions indeed *matter*; pluralists steadily and openly admit that there are real differences between the various world religions, and these differences are *not* inconsequential. Plurality, after all, requires diversity. Unity in spite of the diversity of beliefs is what pluralists of the stripe of Knitter are in pursuit of;

3. All religions have a *mystical* component to them, for, without exception, all world religions describe the "God"—or, better, the Ultimate Reality—that is beyond the scope of full and complete human understanding. If this *Mystery* will never be explored and plundered entirely, then all claims to know It exhaustively are pure idolatry;

---

21. Knitter, *Myth of Religious Superiority*, viii.

22. Knitter, *Myth of Religious Superiority*, ix.

23. These six points are taken, but heavily altered, from Knitter, *Myth of Religious Superiority*, x–xi. Emphasis, however, in the original.

4. Pluralism does *not* imply relativism. While religious pluralists do contend that all religions need to be treated as equally valid, they do not asseverate that all religions are necessarily good . . . or bad. Both helpful and harmful religions and religious practices exist in the world today;

5. The most direly important need from interreligious dialogue is an ethical dialogue among the various religions of the world. The pressing problems of today's world, such as poverty, wars, environmental devastation, and gender injustice, must be broached by a religious pluralism; and

6. In their encounters, even in their dialogues, various religions must respect the freedom of an individual's or a corporate entity's conscience. The instance of "witnessing" must be distinguished from "proselytizing." The former is favorably disposed, whereas the latter is the result of claims to superiority.

In Hick and Knitter's *The Myth of Christian Uniqueness: Toward a Pluralistic Theology of Religions*, Knitter asserts that Christian uniqueness is not meant to be denied per se, but radically reinterpreted instead.

It is that sense of the phrase, *Christian uniqueness*, that the editors and authors dismiss in this title. Knitter asserts that a religiously pluralistic model represents a "paradigm shift" in a Christian theologian's attempt to understand the world of religious diversity, along with Christianity's place within this massive diversity.[24] As we well know from Thomas S. Kuhn, a paradigm shift is something that learns from the past, but is generally different from it, while not completely discarding it. This volume takes Kuhn's understanding of paradigm shift to heart. The starting point for the essays collected here, notes Knitter, is that one must have a *historical consciousness*—that is, the ever more impelling understanding that all knowledge and religious beliefs are historically-culturally conditioned. The second part of this title notes that the *theologico-mystical bridge* between diverse religious traditions is nothing more than *mystery*, which is a point also found in his latter volume in this two-part series, covered

---

24. Hick and Knitter, *Myth of Christian Uniqueness*, vii–ix.

above. The third part of this title emphases the *ethico-practical bridge* among varied religions: that is, justice. Knitter therein himself advocates a position that entails persons of various traditions could—and should—enter into a shared liberative praxis for the poor and suffering, as well as to a shared reflection as to how that praxis relates to their particular religion.[25]

At the beginning of his 2009 book, *Without Buddha I Could Not Be a Christian*, Knitter states that over the last twenty-five years, many Christian beliefs and practices have ceased to make sense to him.[26] The book is an attempt to air his struggles and share the solutions that have helped him hold onto his *modified* Christian faith.[27] In the process, he uses Buddhist concepts to reinterpret basic Christian beliefs and practices. The spiritual project he describes in this book is *double religious belonging*; this term describes the situation in which one is rooted in a primary tradition, but gets substantial support and nourishment from another. In the preface he asks rhetorically whether he is still a Christian and concludes that he thinks he is.

In order to highlight the nourishment that he has received from Buddhism, Knitter adopts the method of "passing over" and "passing back" used by John Dunne in his 1978 book *The Way of All the Earth: Experiments in Truth and Religion*. First, Dunne outlines his struggle with a particular Christian belief or practice. Then he "passes over," which is a process whereby an individual crosses sympathetically from his own religion to another in order to gain insight into how Buddhism deals with the corresponding question. Finally, he "passes back" to Christianity with what he has learned

25. Paul F. Knitter, "Toward a Liberation Theology of Religions," in Hick and Knitter, *Myth of Christian Uniqueness*, 202.

26. Knitter, *Without Buddha*, 4.

27. Importantly, Knitter's contention that he is still a Christian, even though drawing deeply from the wells of Buddhism, is also affirmed by another well-known pluralist scholar of religions: Perry Schmidt-Leukel. Schmidt-Leukel, for example, affirms that he is a Christian, and he is not advocating a new religion in his writings. Instead he wants, as people interact with different cultures and shifting contexts, to stress that changes to one's Christian identity are not necessarily losses but can be opportunities for deepening and positive transformation. Schmidt-Leukel, *Transformation by Integration*, 86.

from Buddhism and in the process reinterprets Christian beliefs based on his new insights. Dunne's own literary odyssey leads him to conclude that all religions are based on common experiences; Knitter concurs. In the first five chapters of *Without Buddha I Could Not Be a Christian* Knitter addresses Christian views about God's transcendence, about God being a personal God, about God and mystery, about heaven and "last things," and about Jesus. For example, in chapter 1, Knitter discusses his difficulties with labeling God as a transcendent other. For him, imaging God as completely separate from creation and human beings inhibits our attempts to be in relationship with God.

Ultimately, God is "Mystery" for Knitter. All the words we use to describe or speak of God are symbols that fail to fully capture the reality of God. In the wordless, imageless silence of Zen meditation, the practitioner moves beyond words to grasp "reality as it really is."[28] Through silence, we open up space to allow "Mystery to speak."[29] It allows us to become aware of the Christ within to which Paul refers to in Gal 2:20. In the end, through such practice, we experience being upheld by what Knitter calls Groundlessness, which means that we accept what is and trust that moment by moment we will be sustained despite letting go of words, images, and thoughts. Knitter reports that this support is real, that it is equivalent to the Christian experience of faith or trust in God, and is the essence of mystical experience. Let us now move to our next thinker, Robert Cummings Neville.

---

28. Knitter, *Without Buddha*, 143.

29. Knitter, *Without Buddha*, 154.

3

Robert Cummings Neville

The Comparative Religious Ideas Project

ROBERT CUMMINGS NEVILLE IS a well-known religious studies scholar at Boston University; he is especially well-known for his comparative theology. He has authored numerous books in the field of comparative religion, including: *The Tao and the Daimon: Segments of a Religious Inquiry* (1981), *Behind the Masks of God: An Essay Toward Comparative Theology* (1991), *Ritual and Deference: Extending Chinese Philosophy in a Comparative Context* (2008), and *Realism in Religion: A Pragmatist's Perspective* (2009). Additionally, Neville is the editor of three volumes that resulted from the Comparative Religious Ideas Project funded by the National Endowment for the Humanities, the Henry Luce Foundation, and Boston University: *The Human Condition, Ultimate Realities*, and *Religious Truth* (all 2001). The latter three texts present a theory of comparison that uses Charles Sanders Peirce's notion of "vagueness" to develop what Neville calls vague categories of comparison. A vague category is any category of thought that is left open to mutually incompatible specifications so as to allow for interpretations that might conflict with each other. Neville argues that the judicious use of such categories enables comparisons to be made in such a way that respects the integrity and diversity of religious traditions. Neville has also penned *Religion in Late Modernity*. More recently, he has authored *Defining Religion: Essays in Philosophy of Religion* (2018). For the sake time and space, I will only be covering two volumes from the above (impressive!) list in what follows: *Religious Truth* and *Defining Religion*. This choice is not only for pragmatic reasons, but also because I deem it true that they are a crystallization of his overarching ideas.

In his more recent title, *Defining Religion*, Neville notes that the concept of defining religion is an immensely difficult one, for to attempt to do so one must make demarcations that others will not agree with. Indeed, everyone, largely, thinks that religion is already defined, yet they almost inherently disagree as to the entailments of the term *religion*. Yet another misconception, in Neville's mind, is that religion is necessarily a Western category, so to impose a definition to it, would be simply to extend the notion of colonialism. However, religion itself is nevertheless a potent and personal force just as much in these days, as in years past. The essays in *Defining Religion* work at defining religion on many levels, and from multifaceted angles. This title was actually written during the years in which Neville was writing his Philosophical Theology three-volume set, as he sensed that he needed to proffer some of the material on a more easily understandable level. With his intention, I contend that he has succeeded. This title is composed of five parts, with the first part named "Heuristics," which is composed of several chapters that cover the nature of the definition of religion, as well as a constructive proposal for what religion might/should mean. Part 2 is titled "Pragmatics," and is composed of a few essays that develop a specifically pragmatic approach to religious experience and the study of religion. The third part is named "Religious Studies," which we will spend the better part of our time upon in this essay of my own, and it explicates the nature of religion with emphasis on comparative studies, the role of philosophy in the study of religion, and the limits of religious naturalism. Part 4 is titled "Philosophical Theology," and ventures to cover what is meant by various first-order issues in philosophical theology, namely conceptions of God, conceptions of creation, and conceptions of what he terms religious worldviews, all the while defending his peculiar notion of "ultimate reality." The fifth part of this collection of essays, "Players," contains essays that concern the contribution to Neville's worldview from John E. Smith, Richard Rorty, William Desmond, and Nancy Frankenberry; we will not concern ourselves at all with part 5 of this text in what follows.

Actual Religion

Moving into the actual text of *Defining Religion* . . . so, what is religion? In defining it, does it allow us to differentiate between what *is* and what *is not* religion? There are manifold types of religion, disciplines studying religion, feelings about religion from "religious" people, etc. So, what is religion exactly? Neville seeks to adjudicate what religion is in part 1 of this text. He stipulates that inquiry into what religion is proceeds more "fruitfully" when one defines religion in a certain manner, so he contends that religion is "the human engagement of ultimacy, which requires harmonizing semiotic cultural systems, aesthetic achievements, social institutions with their own dynamics, and psychological structures" with what is ultimate.[1]

Neville notes that almost everyone assumes that our term *religion* derives from the Latin *religio*. But scholars and people from the past disagree what, exactly, *religio* meant. While Cicero thought that *religio* came from *re-lego*, as in "considering again and again," Lactantius and Augustine thought the word *religio* came from *religo*, which meant "binding together." Notwithstanding, its main meaning in the ancient Roman world was the "scrupulous, strict observance of the services owed to the gods, or to God." For Aquinas, *religio* was a duty owed to God; this "duty" was distorted by the fall, and only Christians have revealed faith which could amend the brokenness—so then, for Aquinas, revealed *religio* was reparative.[2] The point to note here, from this cursory review of the meaning of *religio* in the West, is that from the classical Latin period through even today, the word *religion* has been constantly reworked though

1. Neville, *Defining Religion*, 1.

2. All of this paragraph, heretofore, is roughly based on Neville, *Defining Religion*, 6–7.

the millennia. Indeed, the customary concept of religion came to Western thought, largely, by way of Aristotle's definition of formal causes, in which he describes a hierarchy of genus-species relations with only minor differences distinguishing the various species within a genus.

Neville invites us to suppose, however, that things are not unitary substances, like Aristotle et al. thought, but rather are "harmonies"—that is, some form or pattern unifies the various components of the whole.[3] In fact, because everything is a harmony, everything that composes a harmony is itself a harmony, and so on. One important (and pragmatic!) consequence of defining things as harmonies is that they cannot be defined in and of themselves by only reference to themselves. There must be some sort of existential field in which they interact in order to define things at large, and this is especially the case with religion. Indeed, Neville goes on to assert that religion itself is the "human engagement of ultimacy expressed in cognitive articulations, existential responses to ultimacy . . . and patterns of life and ritual in the face of ultimacy."[4] Neville goes on to discuss five components of this religion, so defined: first are the components having to do with the worship of whatever is taken to be ultimate; second are the components that concern the aesthetic grasp of things as having beauty, or the "special integrity" of harmony. Third are the components that deal with the self, its integration of disparate elements, its overcoming of brokenness with wholeness, and practices of spiritual development. Fourth are the components of social and environmental concern wherein religion takes place. Fifth are the components that concern the cultures, traditions, and trajectories that supply the terms for the conduction of religion. Neville suggests that these five components of religion could be referred to as "worshipful," "aesthetic," "psychological," "environmental," and "semiotic."[5] Each of these, notably, are harmonies of their own, with their own components too. According to

3. Neville, *Defining Religion*, 8.
4. Neville, *Defining Religion*, 9.
5. Neville, *Defining Religion*, 10–11.

Neville, religion is when these components are harmonized insomuch as ultimacy is engaged.

In Neville's view, if religion is harmony, and its components do not harmonize, then that thing is *not* a religion after all. After all, if things are defined as harmonies betwixt other things and not as substances classifiable by their properties, then harmonies are characterized by their relations with one another. For Neville, harmonies are well-construed as "ecological systems" relating to one another.[6] The upshot of this definition is that "harmonies" interdefine things in a whole, not in parts. Neville's pragmatic theory of religion also insists on analyzing religion in its present state, and only then to move backward to its intertwining of roots from earlier stages. He notes that a religious experience is an interpretive engagement of ultimacy structured by hermeneutical intentionality by means of a sign(s) referring to the ultimate object in some context and respect.[7] Further, for Neville, all theology should be comparative theology. All theology, then, should take account of competing religious views. What's more, Neville claims that comparative theology cannot separate itself from what he deems "normative theology" in the systematic sense.[8] Moreover, theology should take as its "public audience" anyone or any discipline or tradition that might contribute to its correction and/or its upbuilding.[9]

Does religion need philosophy? Indeed, says Neville. Although religion has been studied in multiple manners, some of which are fairly devoid of philosophy, Neville supports the integration of philosophy into religion. In fact, he says that "philosophy, in the right sense, is necessary for the definition of religion, which in turn leads to tools for controlling for reductionism in other approaches to the study of religion." Moreover, philosophy is necessary for providing a theory "for understanding and assessing religious symbolism,"[10] which rests within a larger (epistemological) context of engaging

6. Neville, *Defining Religion*, 12.
7. Neville, *Defining Religion*, 95.
8. Neville, *Defining Religion*, 157.
9. Neville, *Defining Religion*, 159.
10. Neville, *Defining Religion*, 165–66.

religious matters. Still further, philosophy is necessary "to give a metaphysical account of the ultimate realities religion engages," an account which "is hypothetical and thus . . . empirical."[11] For Neville, then, religion "is human engagement of ultimacy expressed in cognitive articulations, communal patterns of life or ritual in the face of ultimacy, and personal and communal existential responses to ultimacy that give ultimate definition to the individual and community."[12] One can discern Neville's commitment to pragmatism throughout the above quote, as it is seeping with sentiments from the American pragmatist tradition indeed. He follows Peirce, for example, in contending that we humans are interpreters of reality by means of signs; in fact, we engage reality by interpreting it with and through signs.

Neville and Liberal Theology

Neville also posits a series of recommendations for the future of liberal theology in *Defining Religion*, which are instructive for us to ruminate and cogitate over. The first recommendation is that liberal theology should develop its methods of inquiry in and through the plausibility conditions of the contemporary intellectual situation, i.e., of the twenty-first century. So then, a contemporary liberal theology is, thus, science friendly, by which I mean cognizant of the manifold developments in evolutionary biology. A contemporary liberal theology is also, generally, supernaturalism-hostile. Third, a contemporary liberal theology is ever-looking to develop theories of symbolism that are free from scientific claims. Fourth, a contemporary liberal theology takes seriously the moral claims, entailments, and other various moral elements in religion that emphasize the utter need for piety and justice. Fifth, a contemporary liberal theology gives greater weight to seeking truth in regard to religious topics than to providing identity to a religious group. And finally, a contemporary liberal theology is "open to learning" from as many

---

11. Neville, *Defining Religion*, 165–66.
12. Neville, *Defining Religion*, 166–67.

religions as might teach something, as well as to the multivariate sciences and the secular world.[13]

In fact, as a summary statement of a contemporary liberal theology, Neville proffers that the unifying task of a contemporary liberal theology is the promotion of the Axial Age religious ideals of universal justice, universal compassion, and universal love. So then, in essence, Neville is recommending that a contemporary liberal theology bring to fruition the Axial Age's promise and potential, insomuch as it should seek to connect everything. Additionally, Neville recommends that a contemporary liberal theology adopt wholesale the pragmatic approach to knowledge—that is, one that is fallible (echoing Peirce) and necessarily subject to continual subsequent correction. As a third recommendation, Neville contends that a contemporary liberal theology needs to develop its own metaphysics, and that it needs to do so in conjunction with apophatic theology.[14]

Religious Truth is the second Neville title that I would like to reflect upon in this chapter. It is the concluding volume, the third of three books regarding the Comparative Religious Ideas Project. The three volumes together trace a trajectory of the development of a particular view upon comparative theology. The original intent, ambitious though it was, of this three-volume set was to present the responses to three successive questions (i.e., *The Human Condition*, *Ultimate Realities*, and *Religious Truth*) made by representatives of six major religious traditions. Although the topic of religious truth plays a factor in all of three volumes, this third volume is dedicated foremostly to it, and this third volume also serves as a summary of the preceding two volumes, thereby offering some tentative conclusions on the project as a whole. This, in part, is the reason why I have decided to focus upon this third volume, *Religious Truth*, in this chapter. By the third year of the project, the editors and contributors had settled upon richly nuanced categories of various dimensions of "religious truth." The three categories that they settled upon now follow: (1) The nature of truth as an epistemological problem;

13. Neville, *Defining Religion*, 177.

14. Neville, *Defining Religion*, 182–88.

(2) The expression of truth in the traditions' "scripture(s)," all the while considering authority and revelation; and (3) The cultivation or embodiment of truth.[15]

Although one might automatically think that the best way to categorize religions traditions is phenomenologically, Neville and Wildman suggest that this phenomenological method can be profitably supplemented by four other justifying categories: (1) Accounts of that which is conceptually *feasible* and is capable of explaining why some ideas recur and others do not occur at all; (2) Accounts of the structured relationships among ideas that are capable of explaining why some *transformations* of ideas occur more readily than others; (3) Accounts social, biological, and historical that are capable of explaining why certain religious ideas arose *when*, *where*, and *how* they did; and (4) Accounts of the origins of social, biological, and historical circumstances that are capable of explaining why some religious ideas *transform* in the flux of events in some ways and not others.[16] The first two of these supplements are more conceptual in nature and correspond to insights that are registered in philosophical approaches to comparison, whereas the latter two are more historical and contextual in nature. The purpose of this summary chapter by Neville and Wildman is to, in some cumulative sense, express what religious truth is. They aver, given the complex nature of most religious truth claims, that[17]

- A claim might be true in one context, but not in a slightly different one because all truth claims are concretely instantiated in and by interpretations.

- A claim might be true in its intellectual, but not in its practical interpretation.

15. Robert Cummings Neville and Wesley J. Wildman, "Religious Truth in the Six Traditions: A Summary," in Neville, *Religious Truth*, 146.

16. Robert Cummings Neville and Wesley J. Wildman, "Religious Truth in the Six Traditions: A Summary," in Neville, *Religious Truth*, 146–47.

17. These bulleted statements are all taken from Robert Cummings Neville and Wesley J. Wildman, "Religious Truth in the Six Traditions: A Summary," in Neville, *Religious Truth*, 163–64. They have been massaged a little in order to make them more coherent and concise.

Part I: Four Comparative Religious Theorists

- A claim might be true in its practical, but not in its intellectual entailments.

- A claim might be true in its abstract context, but not in broader contexts.

- A claim might be true in its affect(s) on a community, but not in its theoretical construction, or its relevance for a devotional application.

- A claim might be true in its devotional application, but not in its theory.

- A claim might be true in reference to a particular referent, but not in reference to a slightly different referent.

- A claim might be true in one level of meaning, but not in another level of meaning.

- A claim might be true in its own symbolization isolated from a broader context, but not in its application to other systems.

- A claim might be true in some respects, but not in others.

- A claim might be true in a limited domain of application, but not when generalized.

- A claim might be true generally or vaguely, but not when concretized.

For Neville and Wildman, contemporary understandings of religious truth have come a long way since its eighteenth-century beginnings in philosophy of religion. Developments in twentieth-century philosophy (particularly of language) have complicated the notion of religious truth, from its earlier emphasis upon only epistemological justification. After all, religions use language that is expressive, exhortative, and performative, as well as in ways that are intended to be true in the epistemological sense. As such, religious language can be true or false in special senses, apart from whether it is epistemologically true in its asseverations regarding content. Thus, in all three volumes of the Comparative Religious Ideas Project, but especially in the final volume, the editors and contributors alike are especially concerned with "first-order religious language and activity," with the "conditions of adequacy" that apply to the usage of religious language, and with the religious ideas that "express, cultivate, and regulate those conditions of adequacy" of religious language and practice.[18] All of these lead to the editors' ability to develop a coherent theory of religious truth, one that is not only applicable to truth per se, but also is expandable to understanding the comparative religious project as a whole, for some religious practices might very well involve descriptive claims, whether they be affirmative or negative, but each of these practices has its own "distinctive felicity conditions," such that they comprise "performative felicity," with this latter terminology being preferable because it surmounts the strictly logical entailments of the terminology of "truth" as it has been (over-?)emphasized in Western philosophical epistemology.[19]

Many factors, according to Neville and Wildman, condition the felicity of religious beliefs and practices, and in particular they highlight four dimensions which they consider relevant: (1) How a religious symbol interprets its object to those participants in the practice; (2) Whether a religious symbol actually purports to refer to the reality that it is claimed to; (3) Just what the religious symbol means itself, with all its resonances, ambiguities, etc.; and (4) How the religious interpreters are transformed through the practice in order to grasp its meaning(s).[20] Thus, interpretation, reference, meaning, and transformation are all applicable topics of a theory of religious truth. Particularly, interpretation is the taking of reality by an interpreter to be the way an idea (or sign, see Peirce) says it represents the reality of an object; in a communal context, a religious object is truly interpreted by intellectual symbols that make sense of how the community is religiously shaped, and by practical interpretations that shape that community.[21] Peirce comes

18. Robert Cummings Neville and Wesley J. Wildman, "A Contemporary Understanding of Religious Truth," in Neville, *Religious Truth*, 172–73.

19. Robert Cummings Neville and Wesley J. Wildman, "A Contemporary Understanding of Religious Truth," in Neville, *Religious Truth*, 174.

20. Robert Cummings Neville and Wesley J. Wildman, "A Contemporary Understanding of Religious Truth," in Neville, *Religious Truth*, 176.

21. Robert Cummings Neville and Wesley J. Wildman, "A Contemporary Understanding of Religious Truth," in Neville, *Religious Truth*, 181.

to rescue again regarding the reference factor of religious truth: according to him, there are three kinds of referential truth: iconic, indexical, and conventional.[22] *Iconic* reference, at the most general level, takes reality as what *can* be noticed about it, expressed, and addressed in a particular culture's forms. *Indexical* reference, in contrast, consists of either an idea or sign pointing out something that is otherwise obscured. And *conventional* reference consists in the employment of systems of meaning to proverbially stand for the object in some sense.

For Neville and Wildman, the problem of truth, at least insofar as it applies to the meanings of ideas, is whether or not a religion has a sign or idea that can stand in for the object in a certain respect in such a way that an interpreter is enabled to engage the object interpretively.[23] Without an apropos idea or sign, the object eludes interpretation by the proposed interpreter. Truth in transformation is a carryover of what is important in an object into interpreters in the respect in which ideas (i.e., signs, symbols, theories, etc.) interpret those objects.[24]

So why this seemingly obdurate excursion into Peirce? Well, the Comparative Religious Ideas Project, spearheaded by Neville, has not been about religious "truth" per se, or even "religion," but about "religious ideas" instead. Using this excursion into Peirce and his "ideas," to make a pun on terms, allows Neville (and Wildman) to make some general comments about the nature of religion itself. Religion is, briefly, quite the complex entity. So then, if generalizations about religion in general can be rendered obscure by the mass(es) of details relevant to testing them, then it may be wise to avoid making them. But then, generalizations about and comparisons of religions is what we are all after. So . . . what to do? Well, one must realize precisely the complexity of the religion that s/he

22. Peirce, being the complex and nigh non-understandable thinker that he is, develops his theory of referential meaning in several places, but probably the most clearly in "Speculative Grammar."

23. Robert Cummings Neville and Wesley J. Wildman, "A Contemporary Understanding of Religious Truth," in Neville, *Religious Truth*, 187.

24. Robert Cummings Neville and Wesley J. Wildman, "A Contemporary Understanding of Religious Truth," in Neville, *Religious Truth*, 191–92.

is studying. This is why Neville employed such a complex methodology in his Comparative Religious Ideas Project. He concludes that details that may destroy an overly specific generalization can be considered as specifications of carefully constructed, yet vague, comparative generalizations.[25]

25. Wesley J. Wildman and Robert Cummings Neville, "On the Nature of Religion: Lessons We Have Learned," in Neville, *Religious Truth*, 204–5.

4

David Ray Griffin

Processual Theology

DAVID RAY GRIFFIN WAS professor emeritus of philosophy of religion and theology, Claremont School of Theology and Claremont Graduate University (1973–2004), while concurrently holding the status of co-director, Center for Process Studies. He was also a prolific author. I would, given the empirical data, break up his career into at least "two phases": one pre–9/11/2001, and one post–9/11/2001. Notably, he has written thirty-some-odd books on theology, philosophy, philosophy of religion, and the relation between science and religion. Some of the more notable include *God and Religion in the Postmodern World: Essays in Postmodern Theology*; *Primordial Truth and Postmodern Theology*; *Founders of Constructive Postmodern Philosophy: Peirce, James, Bergson, Whitehead, and Hartshorne*; *Unsnarling the World-Knot: Consciousness, Freedom, and the Mind-Body Problem*; *Reenchantment Without Supernaturalism: A Process Philosophy of Religion*; and *Religion and Scientific Naturalism: Overcoming the Conflicts*. As one can perceive, he was very active pre-2001 with writing titles that had direct bearing on process philosophy and postmodernity.

However, following the events in New York City and elsewhere in September 2001, something changed. He subsequently ventured off into social, ecological and political issues. Indeed, many—about a dozen, actually—of his more recent books have gone off into a different direction than his former titles, and advocate a "truther" position on the events that took place in America on 9/11/2001 and its aftermath through two different political administrations. Nonetheless, he sporadically continued to publish also in his former trajectory; for example: *Two Great Truths: A New Synthesis of Scientific Naturalism and Christian Faith*; *Deep Religious Pluralism*; *Whitehead's Radically Different Postmodern Philosophy: An Argument for Its Contemporary Relevance*; and *God Exists But Gawd Does Not: From Evil to New Atheism to Fine-Tuning*. So then, for the last twenty years or so, Griffin has split his time between numerous nefarious "truther" titles and several more substantive pluralistic and postmodern titles. In this chapter, we will not spend any time on his post-2001 titles, excepting his 2005 title, *Deep Religious Pluralism*.

Significantly, Griffin has coined a number of new terms such as panexperientialism, constructive postmodernism and non-supernatural naturalism. These make important distinctions and contribute to a refinement of thought. He prefers panexperientialism to the more popular panpsychism by asserting that experience is fundamental as a basis for consciousness and freedom that is denied by the prevailing scientific picture. His view is naturalistic without being materialistic, and Griffin is very careful to define various forms of naturalism so as to situate his view within a nondualistic worldview. He proposes a nondualistic, neoanimistic, panexperientialist philosophy in which experience and spontaneity are fully natural features of the world, characteristic of nature at every level. Parapsychology becomes a real possibility in such a view, as does life after death, on which Griffin has written at length; however, he cannot accept the evidence for precognition at face value as he regards it as a contradiction in terms. He upholds the causal efficacy of minds against epiphenomenal views, and exposes the limitations of materialistic philosophical premises.

According to Griffin in his quasi-magnum opus, *Reenchantment Without Supernaturalism: A Process Philosophy of Religion*, there is a core set of ten doctrines shared by the founder of process philosophy, Alfred North Whitehead, and his most able expositor, Charles Hartshorne. For example, (1) In process thought, there is the integration of moral, aesthetic, and religious notions with the general doctrines of the sciences into an internally consistent worldview; (2) In process thought, hardcore commonsense notions are the ultimate test of the coherency of philosophical positions; (3) Whitehead's non-sensationist doctrine of perception, which entails perception to be secondary, is derivative of a more non-sensory "prehension"; (4) In process thought, there is a "panexperientialism with a certain sort of duality," according to which true individuals have at least a miniscule amount of experience, interiority, and spontaneity; (5) In process thought, there is a doctrine that all enduring individuals are serially ordered societies of occasions of experience; (6) Within process thought, there is an assertion that all actual entities have both internal and external relations; (7) Within process thought, there is a naturalistic deism, according to which the divine actuality acts indeed, but variably and never supernaturally within the world; (8) In process thought, there is a doubly dipolar theism in which the divine reality has two aspects or poles; (9) In process thought, one of the chief purposes of our time is the provision of cosmological support for the ideals needed for contemporary civilization; and (10) There is, within process thought, a distinction between verbal statements (i.e., sentences) and propositions, as well as between both of these and propositional feelings.[1]

While Griffin does not limit process thought to these ten principles, he does contend that not one of these ten core doctrines could be eliminated without causing serious damage to the coherence of the process position.[2] As such, process philosophy of religion is one in which a realist, truth-seeking approach is made manifest. Moreover, religious experience founds its discussion in God primarily.[3] Further, a process philosophy of religion is inherently a "revisionary theism," and not a traditional one, that is, one that supports a cross-cultural, many-traditions-based methodology.[4] Griffin notes that the traditional philosophy of religion has been, historically,

1. Griffin, *Reenchantment Without Supernaturalism*, 5–7.
2. Griffin, *Reenchantment Without Supernaturalism*, 3.
3. Griffin, *Reenchantment Without Supernaturalism*, 10.
4. Griffin, *Reenchantment Without Supernaturalism*, 10.

concerned with providing an account of the nature of religion. A process philosophy of religion agrees with this, but disagrees with several others that the traditional account proffers.[5] According to Griffin, all religious activity, no matter who and what it might entail, is an attempt to be in harmony with the ultimate reality.[6] While Christians attempt to be in harmony with their God, Muslims attempt to be in harmony with the will of Allah; Confucians with the mandate of heaven; Taoists with the supreme Tao; Buddhists with nirvana; and so on. That all religions involve a desire to be in touch—and in harmony—with the ultimate reality is a piece of the definition of religion.[7] Full-fledged religions are, according to Griffin, those that consider the ultimate reality holy and sacred; also, full-fledged religions generally picture the natural world as meaningful.[8] A "full-fledged religion" is, for Griffin, a "complex set of beliefs, stories, traditions, emotions, attitudes, dispositions, institutions . . . and practices . . . oriented around the desire to be in harmony with an ultimate reality that is understood to be holy and thereby able to provide life with meaning."[9]

So then, one of the more interesting affirmations of the process philosophy of Griffin is that all major religions are true in a qualified sense.[10] In affirming that all major religions are true in some sense, his version of process philosophy also argues that they must all learn from each other to work towards a religion that more adequately reflects reality. In fact, according to Griffin, process philosophy provides a distinct framework for thinking about the different religious traditions in relation to each other. This distinctiveness flows from two features of process philosophy's naturalistic theism, namely the notion that God himself (*sic!*) is not the only ultimate reality, and that God's power is only expressed in the

5. Griffin, *Reenchantment Without Supernaturalism*, 10.

6. Griffin, *Reenchantment Without Supernaturalism*, 11.

7. Griffin, *Reenchantment Without Supernaturalism*, 12.

8. Griffin, *Reenchantment Without Supernaturalism*, 12.

9. Griffin, *Reenchantment Without Supernaturalism*, 12.

10. Griffin, *Reenchantment Without Supernaturalism*, 247–73.

form of persuasion.[11] That God is not the only ultimate reality is somewhat correlatable to the fact that there are two main types of religion in the world: theistic and nontheistic. So then, it is reflective of the notion that religions, mostly, are divisible into those that worship a personal God, and those that bestow "worthship" (i.e., the etymological foundation of the term *worship*) to an impersonal or "transpersonal" ultimate reality.[12]

Process philosophy, with its naturalistic theism, rules out an exclusivist understanding of religion and salvation, according to which no other religion provides truth and salvation other than Christianity. It also rules out the inclusivist and universalist stance because these two paradigms still insist that the *full* religious truth is possessed by Christians.[13] Because process philosophy insists that ultimate reality is comprised of both God and the notion of creativity, creativity itself is uncreated. In fact, in Whitehead's most careful description of the ultimate, he contends that creativity, the many, and the one all comprise the notion of "being."[14] In Hartshorne's view, God is essentially the soul of the universe; his very nature in being God is to unite the multiplicities constituting the universe. In Griffin's extrapolation, God is the *in-formed* ultimate, and creativity is the *formless* ultimate.[15] Thus, in so doing, process philosophy provides the basis for a version of religious pluralism, which segues into our next topic regarding the corpus of Griffin.

Whiteheadian religious pluralism undermines the idea that theistic religions, largely, are right, and that nontheistic religions are just plain wrong. In its stead, Whiteheadian religious pluralism serves as the basis for mutual respect betwixt different religions, and even different (non-)theisms. Moreover, this Whiteheadian religious pluralism also supports the "cosmic optimism" of the full-fledged religions mentioned earlier.[16] Having said this, let us, then,

11. Griffin, *Reenchantment Without Supernaturalism*, 248.

12. Griffin, *Reenchantment Without Supernaturalism*, 248.

13. Griffin, *Reenchantment Without Supernaturalism*, 256.

14. Griffin, *Reenchantment Without Supernaturalism*, 260–61.

15. Griffin, *Reenchantment Without Supernaturalism*, 261.

16. Griffin, *Reenchantment Without Supernaturalism*, 284.

consider the entailments of Griffin's most complete thought upon the ideas of religious pluralism as found in his volume entitled *Deep Religious Pluralism*.

Whereas "religious diversity" refers to the straightforward stipulation that there are numerous religious traditions, "religious pluralism" refers to "beliefs and attitudes." As such, religious pluralists do not believe that their own religion is the only legitimate one; instead, they contend that there are positive values and truths—salvation even!—provided by a plurality of different religious traditions. Griffin's book, *Deep Religious Pluralism*, is founded upon the idea that Whitehead's cosmology and philosophy encourage not only religious pluralism, but *deep* religious pluralism at that. Griffin offers this as a corrective to Western theological bends, quasi-recently, that have been evoking a rejection of pluralism as such. The distinctive perspective herein is that if religious pluralism is approached from a strong Whiteheadian position, more satisfactory results can be attained than without it. This book endeavors to show that a Whiteheadian approach to religious pluralism articulates a position that is deeply pluralistic (hence the title), and that this approach allows Christians to articulate a form of religious pluralism that does not undermine the distinctive truths and values of the Christian faith. It also seeks to demonstrate that this Whiteheadian pluralistic approach can help theologians—and philosophers of religion—from various other traditions to articulate forms of religious pluralism that do not deny their individual tradition's truths or values either.[17]

To accept a form of religious pluralism entails an adherent to a particular tradition to both deny something and affirm something: to deny religious absolutism and to affirm the notion that there are indeed religions other than their own that provide legitimacy in their pursuit(s) of truth and value. *Deep Religious Pluralism* is based upon fundamental ideas that are five in number: one, that religious plurality is indicative of the state of the world today, and as such, the acceptance of religious pluralism is "vitally important"; two, the growth of religious pluralism is *now* "especially important" to Christians, be they nominal or vociferous in their advocacy of

17. Griffin, *Deep Religious Pluralism*, xiii–xiv.

the tenets of Christianity, because Christians' power in the present milieu—comprised of military might, economic dominance, and cultural preeminence—is growing, seemingly year over year; three, the Christian West has taken a "wrong turn" in that it falsely claims that a religiously pluralistic position posits a "neutral" universality, that it is not "really Christian," that it is not even truly pluralistic, and that it entails a "debilitating relativism"; fourth, Whiteheadian philosophy provides a basis for understanding and articulating a clearly Christian pluralism of religions that does *not* pretend an "impossible neutrality," that is "truly" pluralistic, and that avoids a "debilitating relativism"; and fifth, Whiteheadian philosophy truly and realistically provides a basis for patrons from other religious traditions than Christianity to postulate a pluralism that would be helpful to their fellow adherents.[18]

As aforenoted in this present essay, in 1983 Alan Race provided the original typology that (still) predominates topics regarding religious plurality in the world today: that is, positions are either exclusivistic or inclusivistic.[19] Race mentioned, at the time, four individuals in the then-contemporary religious scene as religious pluralists: Paul Tillich, John Hick, Wilfred Cantwell Smith, and John B. Cobb. In the more recent discussions of pluralism, Tillich has been supplanted by Paul F. Knitter, about whom this essay has expounded upon earlier (I will end my reflections in this essay, though, with a *return* to Tillich). Griffin avers that all of these thinkers, though they may differ on the particulars, promote a sort of "generic pluralism," by which religious pluralism is being driven by sociological, theological, ethical, and ontological concerns.

A twofold change in the sociological aspects of Christianity have occurred in the twentieth century, for example: one side of this change is that there is now much more knowledge of other religions, than in past eras; the second side of this sociological change is based upon the fundamental recognition that the Christian faith has come to be pictured as *more* morally culpable, *more* imperialistic,

18. Griffin, *Deep Religious Pluralism*, 3–4.

19. See Race, *Christians and Religious Pluralism*, 71, 88, 98.

and *less* spiritual than other religions.[20] Another basis for this shift to religious pluralism, according to Griffin herein, is a theological judgment that the doctrine of love is primary. In view of such, absolutism is to be abhorred. A third basis for this shift is more ethical in orientation: modern religious pluralists contend that there are highly destructive effects from insisting on Christian superiority. In its stead, this move in recent years toward a more fully religious pluralism is, seemingly, based upon the Christian imperative to love one's neighbor. Ontologically, the rejection of supernaturalism and the embrace of naturalism has also given impetus toward the revival of religious pluralism in the contemporary world.

20. Griffin, *Deep Religious Pluralism*, 8–9.

5

Roland Faber

God as the Manifold Poet

ROLAND FABER WAS, PRIOR to his retirement in 2022, Kilsby Family/
John B. Cobb Jr. Professor of Process Studies at Claremont School
of Theology, professor of religion and philosophy at Claremont
Graduate University, executive co-director of the Center for Process
Studies, and executive director of the Whitehead Research Project.
He has published or edited roughly two dozen books in English and
another dozen in German. Some of his more notable publications
(non-edited) include the following titles pertinent to this chapter,
which demonstrate his proficiency in process philosophy and the
broad category of comparative religion: *God as Poet of the World:
Exploring Process Theologies*, which is probably his most significant
book to date (for me, anyway), but we will not have the time or
space to cover it, unless only tangentially; *The Divine Manifold*; *The
Becoming of God: Process Theology, Philosophy, and Multireligious
Engagement*; *The Garden of Reality: Transreligious Relativity in a
World of Becoming*; and, most recently, *The Ocean of God: On the
Transreligious Future of Religions*.

Because of the focused orientation of this present chapter, I
will be reflecting upon only one title by Faber: *The Ocean of God: On
the Transreligious Future of Religions*. *The Ocean of God* begins with
a rhetorical question that somewhat guides the remainder of the

book: paraphrasing, "how can the different religions in the contemporary world relate to each other (and sometimes themselves) in a mutually edifying manner?" The answer to this question regards the meaning of human experience, and the destiny of humanity.[1]

For all of the potential fissures and fractions in today's world, especially when viewed through a religious prism, Faber herein advocates that two concepts and ways of thinking may ease the friction and actually promote overall well-being in the world today: the healing prescription of religious pluralism (or multiplicity),[2] and the unity of religions.[3] Into this situation, Faber contends that Whitehead's philosophy, veritably from its inception, has generated a multiplicity of pluralistic approaches to interreligious dialogue. It has, in Faber's words, proven itself to be a "contact theory" that can "bridge" religious identities, for it has generated multiplicitous arguments for religious pluralism "from the perspective of, and embedded in," the diversity of religious traditions.[4] Faber notes that religious plurality is a fact of our world today, and probably always has been in the past too;[5] this plurality, in and of itself, is not problematic per se. However, "the heritage it has left for our common world today and the impact it has had on human existence and [our] evolution in the past" has been at times; indeed, as Faber puts it, it has oft left us with "Feelings of a cauldron of dissention, disagreement, violence and mutual destruction."[6]

Notably, Faber avers that with the "postmodern" situation, with the rise of "new age" religions, religion has gained new currency as a transformed and transformative category of new interlinked spiritual realities that cannot be reduced to the reductionisms of

1. Faber, *Ocean of God*, 1.

2. Faber herein uses the term "multiplicity" to indicate a field of mutual immanence or foldings in the sense of Gilles Deleuze. See Faber, *Divine Manifold*, chap. 8.

3. Faber, *Ocean of God*, 2.

4. Faber, *Ocean of God*, 3.

5. Wallace, in 1966, a little over fifty years ago, estimated that the world has seen, over its duration, about 100,000 different religions. See Wallace, "Rituals: Sacred and Profane."

6. Faber, *Ocean of God*, 13.

the past, especially its view of the "world religions." Faber uses the term "religion(s)" in this sense, noting that it refers to the multiplicity and unity of religions, which he also designates "transreligious horizon[s]." For Faber, transreligious discourse identifies its dynamic as a "movement and flow" within and between religions that is "justified by the myriads of factual creative receptions, borrowings, reformulations, recalibrations, imitations, [and] receptions . . . of conceptualizations, doctrines, teachings, lifestyles, behavioral patterns, rituals, [and] ideas . . . of different cultures and religious traditions."

Moreover, transreligious is a "prescriptive category of analysis, comparison, transformation, and synthesis that restates the very intellectual basis for the claims of religious pluralism and the unity of religions."[7] This transreligious discourse pictures and perceives these multireligious flows as expressions of both truth and the ultimate reality itself through which humanity may gain the peace of, within, and between radically different (and not so radically different!) religious traditions, which Faber considers to be the "spiritual maturity of humanity."[8] In fact, Faber writes that the unity of religions is one of the markers of the new type of religions and movements that have appeared in the last couple of centuries. Faber's thesis within *The Ocean of God* is that the future of religions will either be transreligious, or there will be *no humanity* to have religious discourse at all.

Indeed, the title *The Ocean of God* itself provokes within one the sense of this transreligious "essence" of religions and indicates their future with the terminology of "ocean," which has been used variously and at various times throughout religious history to express the depths of God. Faber continues, "The unbounded ocean [that] vibrates [as a sea] of God's love, grace [and] mercy . . . always celebrating the overflowing unity and multiplicity of the Mystery" is an illustrative metaphor.[9] Indeed, the ocean is vast, spacious, undifferentiated, fascinating, unknown and unknowable at the same

7. Faber, *Ocean of God*, 7.
8. Faber, *Ocean of God*, 7–8.
9. Faber, *Ocean of God*, 8.

time, and inherently unpredictable and even dangerous. This is definitely an apropos metaphor for God! Faber, in my words, means that divine revelation pours forth moisture and nourishment to the masses as "divine revelation rains down from the divine clouds,"[10] and the multiplicity of religions may indeed be, again metaphorically, the proverbial rivers seeking union with the all-consuming ocean, which could then evaporate, condense, and start the process all over again.

The so-called "Axial Age" phrase originated with the German psychiatrist and philosopher Karl Jaspers, who noted that during this period there was a shift—or a turn, as if on an axis—away from more predominantly localized concerns and toward *transcendence*.[11] Axial Age thinkers displayed great originality and yet exhibited surprising similarity with respect to their ultimate concerns.[12] Numerous "religions" arose and or concretized during this time frame. Bellah and Joas note that by seeing the Axial Age as the period of the emergence of formative traditions of religious and philosophical thought they are not implying that culture began in the Axial Age per se or that what went before it can be ignored. Nevertheless, the Axial Age is only intelligible in terms of what went before it: a very long and very significant history in which human culture emerged as a way of relating to the world shared by no other animal.[13]

To date, most theorists have suggested that the nature of the axial change was cognitive or intellectual. In particular, it has often been argued that, during the Axial Age, people began to be more "reflexive."[14] The moment a society becomes aware of its contingency it questions itself and change can happen. In this text, Bellah considers this the beginning of the period called the Axial Age. Notably, Jaspers originally defined reflexivity as "general consciousness" and as "thinking about thinking": Jaspers notes, "Hitherto unconsciously

10. Faber, *Ocean of God*, 9.

11. See Jaspers, *Origin and Goal of History*. See also Bellah and Joas, "Introduction," in *Axial Age and Its Consequences*, 1.

12. Bellah and Joas, *Axial Age and Its Consequences*, 1.

13. Bellah and Joas, "Introduction," in *Axial Age and Its Consequences*, 2.

14. See Eisenstadt, *Origins and Diversity*.

accepted ideas, customs and conditions were subjected to examination, questioned and liquidated."[15] This radical questioning of tradition led, he claims, to monotheism in the eastern part of the Mediterranean and to the birth of philosophy in its western part. As local and tradition-specific as their investigations may have begun, their concerns were global, even universal.[16] As such, the appearance of thinkers who still are a source of inspiration for present-day religious and spiritual movements mark the (first) Axial Age: for example, Socrates, Pythagoras, Buddha, Mahavira, Confucius, Lao Tse, the Hebrew prophets, etc.[17] The (first) Axial Age has recently been the focus of increasing interest, but its existence is still very much in dispute as a matter of fact.[18] The main reason for questioning the existence of the Axial Age is that its nature, as well as its spatial and temporal boundaries, remain very much unclear. The standard explanation to the (first) Axial Age defines it as a change of cognitive style, from a narrative and analogical style to a more analytical and reflective style, probably due to the increasing use of external memory tools. But Baumard et al. proffer that a change in reward orientation, from a short-term materialistic orientation to a long-term spiritual one, was the proximate cause of the Axial Age.[19] I think these both can be true.

That little aside being cursorily mentioned, let us return to Faber's text. Faber notes that the "first" Axial Age was characterized by the global awakening of humanity by a "universal consciousness of existence to a world in need of salvific or healing transformation." Building upon this insight, Faber contends that a "new" Axial Age, that is, the centuries around the turn from the second to the third millennium, "has awakened humanity to a different universal consciousness, namely, that of the mutual interrelatedness of humanity."[20] Issuing forth from the derivation of this new Axial Age,

15. Jaspers, *Origin and Goal of History*, 10.

16. Truncated, abbreviated, and summarized from *Encyclopedia Britannica*. Stefon, "Axial Age."

17. Jaspers, *Origin and Goal of History*, 10.

18. Cf. Armstrong, *Great Transformation*.

19. Baumard et al., "What Changed During the Axial Age."

20. Faber, *Ocean of God*, 15.

religious pluralism is an endeavor that seeks to "encompass religious diversity in one universal framework of the spiritual development of humanity." This polyphilic pluralism has "become fully possible as . . . a universal consciousness [of the desire for] unity has . . . arisen." For the "new paradigm" of religious pluralism, this unity can be developed by the "unfettered evaluation of the *plurality* of religions."[21] This (second) Axial Age "fuses the becoming of the cosmos with that of mind and spirit . . . not *away from* the world, but *deeper into* it; not as salvation venturing *beyond* the world . . . but as ripening fruit or harvest of the world process *itself*."[22] Faber goes on to project that the "decisive character of the 'surviving' religiosity of the future is its *relationality* . . . and *forms of unification* [that will] surpass any human particularities of cultural difference."[23] The very unity of religions, Faber anticipates, will be sustained by patterns of human involvement in the cosmic becoming of humanity itself.

Herein Faber critiques several views of the pluralistic positions we have on tap today: what he refers to as the "monocentric-differential (apophatic)" (what I will refer to below as MDA) view; the "polycentric-differential (cataphatic)" (PDC) view; the "monocentric-relational (apophatic)" (MRA) view; and the "polycentric-relational (cataphatic)" (PRC) view. Notably, Faber points out that our previous dialogue partner in this essay, Paul Knitter, is an example of the first modality of the differential-relational matrix, what I have dubbed the MDA view, or shorthandedly referred to as the monocentric apophatic approach. Knitter, as such, delineates between two possible outcomes of a normalization of pluralistic views: either the "permanent mutuality" of religious diversity, or, alternatively, the "persistent acceptance" of the otherness of religions. The first option, i.e., what Faber dubs the permanent mutuality view, would mean that religions remain within their distinct heritage of origination, but would engage infinitely in dialogue; the second option, i.e., what Faber calls the persistent acceptance view, would mean that the various religions would accept the "unbridgeable

21. Faber, *Ocean of God*, 16–17. Emphasis in original.
22. Faber, *Ocean of God*, 18.
23. Faber, *Ocean of God*, 19. Emphasis in original.

differences" of the many religions—its aim would not be mutuality, but diversity instead. However, according to Faber, Knitter realizes that universality per se is not finality, which constitutes for Faber, a proverbial Knitterian crossing into the unity of religions.[24]

A second modality of the differential-relational matrix is what I have referred to above as the PDC. S. Mark Heim would be a representative of this polycentric cataphatic approach. Heim would, seemingly, suggest that different religions have different paths toward "salvation" (however defined), but also that they have entirely different aims. That is, the Buddhist explores intently for nirvana, the Jewish/Christian for salvation and redemption, etc. In this model, as per Faber, the individual would receive their desire for ultimacy by following the path laid out by their particular religious tradition, and not by some amalgamated final end state. Heim does, however, introduce a sort of trinitarian mutuality into his conceptioning, which in my opinion totally mitigates the thrust of his contentions, and that for the negative.[25]

A third modality of the differential-relational matrix, MRA, focuses on the apophatic-relational propositions of the "salvation/liberation/ultimate fulfillment" desire of humanity. John Hick is an excellent exponent of this view, and his influence redounds to almost every level of scholarship in religious pluralism today. His most enduring contribution might very well be that many religious traditions agree that *ultimate reality* is, at base level, "inaccessible, inexplicable, hidden, and unknown."[26] In other words, ultimate reality is forever unknowable, and forever unknown in its essence. Or, in traditional terms, ultimacy is apophatic in nature. As Faber indicates, the drawbacks of Hick's position are numerous: for example, the application of a Kantian worldview by Hick allows "Hick to postulate the utter unknowability of Reality in itself (the noumenal)," but it has the converse action of making ultimate reality not to be engaged in anything in the phenomenal world.[27]

---

24. Faber, *Ocean of God*, 32–33.
25. Faber, *Ocean of God*, 33–34.
26. Faber, *Ocean of God*, 35.
27. Faber, *Ocean of God*, 36.

A fourth conception of the differential-relational matrix comes from Alfred North Whitehead's thought, or at least the application of his thought, one which I have labeled above PRC. This proposal, advocated by the likes of John B. Cobb and David Ray Griffin (also a conversation partner above in this essay) suggests a "deep religious pluralism," by which other religionists fail to be "deep enough," either being constrained by their limitation to insights from one religion or "being confined by a pluralism that fails in light of a quest for knowledge to finding some type of unity, harmony, or coherence."[28] While this is Faber's own tradition of thought, he does not subscribe to such a model outright; he develops his pluralistic alternative into a different flavor of Whiteheadianism.

28. Faber, *Ocean of God*, 37.

PART II

Praxis Beyond Method and Theory

6

From Method to Praxis

Wilfred Cantwell Smith and Paul Tillich

Faith is the state of being ultimately concerned: the
dynamics of faith are the dynamics of man's ultimate
concern.[1]

MANY YEARS AGO, WILFRED Cantwell Smith stated that we had
arrived at yet another of a continuing series of Copernican Revo-
lutions in our theological thinking: having tried to settle its accounts with geology, historical criticism, and evolutionary biology,
Christian theology must begin to reckon with "the faith of other
men"; he gallantly proclaims that the religious life of humankind
from now on, if it is to be lived at all, will be lived in a context
of religious pluralism.[2] After all, according to him, it will become
increasingly apparent, and is already essentially true, that to be a
Christian in the modern world, or a Jew, or an agnostic, is to be so
in a society in which others, intelligent, devout, and righteous, are

1. Tillich, *Dynamics of Faith*, 14.
2. Smith, *Patterns of Faith*, 22.

Buddhists, Muslims, Hindus.[3] It is both easier and more difficult for theologians, as Smith urges they must, to abandon their isolationism along with the notion that other religions are simply great mistakes—and their followers deluded. Smith wrote regretfully that he had to place Paul Tillich in this category of outmoded "exclusivists." This is rather surprising, and Smith himself seemed to see some hope of modifying this judgment with the late appearance of Tillich's *Christianity and the Encounter of the World Religions*.[4] In fact, I contend that there were already important elements in Tillich's writings indicating a substantially broader perspective on the other world religions than Smith was able to recognize, as evident in Tillich's views upon faith, belief, and religion itself.

The modern student of religion may look upon religion as something that other people do, or she may see and feel it as something in which also she herself is also involved. In either case, she approaches any attempt to understand it conscious not only of the many traditional problems, but also of new complications.[5] Several of these new complications—such as providentialism—will be covered in what follows below, while others—for example the onslaught from the biological sciences—will only be given short shrift. But before we get into either the problems with faith or belief, let us first discover what the following two men—Paul Tillich and Wilfred Cantwell Smith—have to say about the generic concept of "religion." But before we get into the individual authors, perhaps it is wise to briefly mention several questions: What is religion, or a religion? What is religious faith? What is religious belief? Such questions, asked either from the outside or from within, must nowadays be set in a wide context.

Smith's method to understand religion, belief, and faith begins with simply a verbal inquiry, for the way that we use words is a significant *index* of how we humans think. Also, more actively, it is a significant factor in *determining* how we think.[6] To understand

3. Smith, *Patterns of Faith*, 23–24.
4. Smith, *Faith of Other Men*, 111–12.
5. Smith, *Meaning and End of Religion*, 7.
6. Smith, *Meaning and End of Religion*, 19.

the world, and ourselves, it is helpful if we in the contemporary context become critical of the terms and concepts that we are using. Further, to understand other people and other ages, it is requisite that we in the contemporary context do not presume uncritically that their meanings for words are the same as our contemporary ones. A mature history of ideas must rest on a careful scrutiny of new words, and also of new developments in meanings for old words. Once attained, it may further our realistic understanding of the world itself. Three levels are here involved for Smith: First, there are the words that men use; second, there are the concepts in their minds, of which these words are the more or less effective expression; third, there is the real world, some aspects of which the concepts are the more or less adequate representation.[7] Smith asserts that we must be alert lest, out of casualness or lack of historical perception, we fail to notice changes in word usage that may be quite significant, so that we read back into the past what are actually our innovations; we must be alert also lest we fail to grasp how the ideas behind even the same words vary, in subtle or profound ways, from thinker to thinker, from century to century, from community to community—so that we read into other people's minds ideas out of our own context. Finally, we must be alert lest the concepts that either they or we have in our minds be taken as axiomatically valid, so that we read our ideas into the universe rather than vice versa.[8]

The surest way to misunderstand a great religious tradition is to miss its profundity.[9] After all, many important concepts to us humans such as "revelation" or "redemption," or even "salvation," generally speak of an action that happens only once, an action that is transcendent in orientation, and an action that is transformative in its effect on reality; contrast this with the concept of "religion," wherein the term subordinates a whole panoply of spiritual acts under a general concept.[10] *Religion* is a human action, whereas "revelation," "redemption," and "salvation," speak of divine action,

---

7. Smith, *Meaning and End of Religion*, 19.

8. Smith, *Meaning and End of Religion*, 20–21.

9. Smith, *Patterns of Faith*, 30.

10. Tillich, *What Is Religion?*, 27.

or what I have termed in my dissertation, "divine involvement" or "divine activity." Having set this first thesis forth, let us delve into what Tillich and Smith state about the concept of religion.

Multivariousness Exemplified: Tillich and Smith on Religion

Let us consider first the word and the concept *religion* itself: the term is notoriously difficult to define. At least, there has been in recent decades a bewildering variety of definitions; and no one of them has commanded wide acceptance.[11] In some cases of this sort, a repeated failure to agree, to reach any satisfying answer or even to make any discernible progress towards one, has turned out to mean that people have been asking a wrong question. In this instance one might argue that the sustained inability to clarify what the word *religion* signifies in itself suggests that the term ought to be dropped, that it is a distorted concept not really corresponding to anything definite or distinctive in the objective world.[12]

Smith notes that what we call religion is of much wider prevalence and of much longer standing than is the use of this term, or indeed of any other term, to designate it. In every human community on earth today there exists something that we, as sophisticated observers, may term religion, or a religion. And we are able to see it in each case as the latest development in a continuous tradition that goes back, we can now affirm, for at least one hundred thousand years. Humanity is everywhere and has always been what we today call *religious*, yet there are today and have been in the past relatively few languages into which one can translate the word *religion*—and even fewer its plural, *religions*—outside Western civilization.[13] The word religion is originally from the Latin *religio*, a term that eventually was used in a great variety of senses, even by a single writer, without precision. So then, this much at least is clear: that people throughout history and throughout the world have been able to be

---

11. Smith, *Meaning and End of Religion*, 21.
12. Smith, *Meaning and End of Religion*, 21.
13. Smith, *Meaning and End of Religion*, 22.

religious without the assistance of a special term, like the word *religion* itself.[14] Oaths, family proprieties, cultic observances and the like were each *religio* to a person; or, showing the ambivalence, one could equally say that to break a solemn oath is *religio*, that is, is taboo—as we might say, is sacrilegious.[15]

The next great development in the concept of religion, according to Smith, was a radical one. In the next few centuries something quite new in this realm emerged in the Mediterranean world, and eventually dominated it: namely, a systematic and organized community, which modernity looking back designates as the religion of Christianity. It was new not only in content but in form, for the Christian community introduced a quite new notion covering a quite new phenomenon, that of "church." According to Smith, the concept of religion did not altogether keep pace with the new evolution. The Christian group, to verbalize the new life that they were experiencing and proclaiming, introduced in addition to *ecclesia* other new vocabulary as well, the most important of which was the new concept "faith."[16] A distinguishing mark of the new *faith* was that it ramified into every aspect of the believer's life, moral, social, intellectual, as well as liturgical, in a way that was quite new. One consequence was that the term *religio*, once the Christians adopted it, quickly became more multifaceted than ever, and took on quite new depths, but it gained nothing in clarity.[17]

Augustine is the last writer before the Renaissance to evince a significant interest in the concept of *religio*, and upon it he wrote a book (i.e., *De Vera Religione*), which was the first time that a Christian writer had undertaken to explicate a notion of *religio* rather than using the term somewhat incidentally.[18] In the contemporary context we oft translate the title of this work as "On the True Religion" and suppose that the writer, since he is known to have been a Christian, would believe that the true religion is Christianity. But this

14. Smith, *Meaning and End of Religion*, 22.
15. Smith, *Meaning and End of Religion*, 23–24.
16. Smith, *Meaning and End of Religion*, 27–28.
17. Smith, *Meaning and End of Religion*, 28–29.
18. Smith, *Meaning and End of Religion*, 30.

would be a misrendering. A better approximation of what Augustine meant by the title would be something along the lines of "On True Religion," with the idea being referent to the order of "On Proper Piety" or "On Genuine Worship."[19] The book argues at great length and in many ways that *vera religio* means the worship of the one true God; notably, it hardly mentions Christianity, and culminates in a warm, reverberating, and sustained affirmation of a personal relation to that transcendent God. For Augustine, *religion* is no system of observances or beliefs, nor an historical tradition, institutionalized or susceptible of outside observation, but a vivid and personal confrontation with the splendor and the love of God instead.[20] The culmination is mystic, for he is arguing rather that mankind's true nature is fulfilled in a close personal engagement with the divine, and that Christ has made this possible. With this title, there is a new idea in this phrase, "true" religion, one that made possible the transition to the later institutionalized meaning. Indeed, this led at last to the concept that one religion (in a later sense) is true, others false—a major turning point in the history of humanity.[21]

Smith notes that after Augustine the word *religio* was little used. If the salient point about the early fathers' use of *religio* is its rich diversity, it is notable that throughout the Catholic Middle Ages this particular term was little employed. For the medieval church, the great word was always *faith*. The one sense of the term *religio* that is found fairly steadily through the Middle Ages is a development from the meaning "rite," namely the specialized designation of the monastic life as *religio*. Similarly in the other, daughter languages, the first meaning of *religion* in English, in the *Oxford Dictionary*, is "a state of life bound by monastic vows," testified by AD 1200.[22] The term also designated a particular monastic or religious order or rule, and it is in this sense also that Aquinas chiefly uses the word, though he touches on it briefly in its more general significance also. For him

19. Smith, *Meaning and End of Religion*, 30–31.
20. Smith, *Meaning and End of Religion*, 30–31.
21. Smith, *Meaning and End of Religion*, 32.
22. Smith, *Meaning and End of Religion*, 33.

it is also an activity of the soul: it is the person of faith's prompting towards the due worship of God.[23]

Moving into the Enlightenment, according to Smith, *religio* became referent to a "system of ideas," and of "beliefs."[24] Religion as a systematic entity, as it emerged in the seventeenth and eighteenth centuries, is a concept of polemics and apologetics. Smith sums up this period by noting that we may say that some Renaissance humanists and then some Protestant Reformers adopted a concept of religion to represent an inner piety; but that in the seventeenth and early eighteenth centuries this was largely superseded by a concept of schematic externalization that reflected, and served, the clash of conflicting religious parties, the emergence of a triumphant intellectualism, and the emerging new information from beyond the seas about the patterns of other men's religious life. These provided the foundations of the concept for the modern world.[25]

But in the later eighteenth and early nineteenth centuries, due in part to the influence of John Wesley, there was a movement of return to a reemphasis on a richer and more personal and more moral attitude.[26] Later, as a result of Schleiermacher's influential work, and of the whole romantic movement that it exemplified, there was a shift of meaning of the term *religio* back to the inward and nonintellectual part of the religious life.[27] The rather "recent" meeting of religious faith with rationalistic and then scientific inquiry, and the increasing meeting among diverse traditions of faith, have led to a temporary confusion of terms and beclouding of issues.[28] In sum, for Smith, life itself, the end of religion, in the classical sense of its purpose and goal, that to which it points and may lead, is God.[29] What a person thinks about religion is central to what he thinks about life and the universe as a whole, at least according to Smith,

---

23. Smith, *Meaning and End of Religion*, 33.

24. Smith, *Meaning and End of Religion*, 40.

25. Smith, *Meaning and End of Religion*, 43–44.

26. Smith, *Meaning and End of Religion*, 44.

27. Smith, *Meaning and End of Religion*, 45.

28. Smith, *Meaning and End of Religion*, 19.

29. Smith, *Meaning and End of Religion*, 181.

and the meaning that one ascribes to the term is a key to the meaning that one finds in existence.[30]

For Tillich, religions were never a matter of rational knowledge; they were not appraisable in terms of general experience. Each religion had, or has, its own center which must be received by faith. There is no religion with a capital R, one may infer from Tillich: all religions come for faith in their own circles of worship, interpretation and application, and in terms of the nature of their own distinctive, ultimate concern. All statements of religion are theological, not ontological, and must be formulated, expressed and communicated in terms of symbols for faith. But no religion is more than symbolic and, therefore, as Tillich states, concrete religions serve the worshiper to provide a set of symbols for ultimate concern only in such a way that if the symbols pale or lose meaning it is quite all right to abandon one set of symbols in order to accept another which provides more power for vivid experience: all religions are relative, and therefore there is no loss of truth in the change of religions.[31] Tillich insists that the symbols participate in the reality which they symbolize.[32]

The outsider students of religion, in their attempt at explanation, must reckon with the fact that, despite all "debunking," people find in religion something outweighing the critics' charges. From within, the person of religion must strive to attain some exposition of that religion that will do justice to the values that, even in the modern world, are being made available to them. Though this continuing or renewed vitality is general, it is also particular. One has not understood religion if one's interpretation is applicable to only one of its forms. On the other hand, neither has one understood religion if one's interpretation does justice only to some abstraction of religiousness in general but not to the fact that for most people of faith, loyalty and concern are not for any such abstraction but quite specifically and perhaps even exclusively for their own unique

30. Smith, *Meaning and End of Religion*, 21.

31. Tillich, *Dynamics of Faith*, 46.

32. Tillich, *Dynamics of Faith*, 47.

tradition—or even for one section within that.[33] For Smith, it is common nowadays to hold that there is in human life and society something distinctive called *religion* and that this phenomenon is found on earth at present in a variety of minor forms, chiefly among outlying or eccentric peoples, and in a half dozen or so major forms. Each of these major forms is also called "a religion," and each one has a name: Christianity, Buddhism, Hinduism, and so on.[34]

Tillich's understanding of the essential is the only foundation of his contention that humanity is universally endowed with faith consciousness, that is, faith as ultimate concern. The universal basis of humanity's ultimate concern is its universal experience of the essential from which it feels its estrangement and to which it is driven as to the recovery of its truth as grounded in God. Through his essentialism, Tillich can thus identify the universality of guilt or estrangement as the sense of something radically amiss in existential humanity distanced, though never severed, from its essence, and also identify the deepest and universal experience of human eros as the drive to recover that essence from which humanity is removed in existence. In the same essentialist logic, history becomes the search for the essential and so all of history becomes the history of religion culminating in the *kairotic* moment or moments when the meaning of history is revealed in the epiphanies of the essential. The essential–existential relationship thus allows Tillich to give precise philosophical description to humanity's universal religious instinct and so to honor the variety of humanity's religions even if, as in his earlier Christian provincialism, these religions are somehow ordered to the Christ event.

In defining religion, which he regarded as "the substance, the ground and the depth of man's spiritual life,"[35] Tillich employed the term *ultimate concern*. Religion, or faith, he said, is the state of being grasped by the power of being itself, by an unconditional concern or by that which concerns one unconditionally. This is Tillich's own definition, though it sounds very much like Luther's famous

33. Smith, *Meaning and End of Religion*, 9.
34. Smith, *Meaning and End of Religion*, 19.
35. Tillich, *Theology of Culture*, 8.

interpretation: "Faith is the state of being grasped by that which concerns one unconditionally."[36] For Tillich, religion is the state of being grasped by an ultimate concern, a concern that qualifies all other concerns as preliminary and which itself contains the answer to the question of the meaning of life. For Schleiermacher, the essence of religion consists in the feeling of absolute dependence. The union of subject and object in Tillich's concept of faith finds a relative continuity with Schleiermacher's idea of "feeling of absolute dependence." In the same way as Tillich, Schleiermacher's goal was a synthesis of subjective experience and objective reality.[37] Tillich himself claims that "Schleiermacher's 'feeling of absolute dependence' was rather near to . . . 'ultimate concern.'"[38]

However, faith and religion are not just feelings for Tillich. "The word 'feeling' has induced many people to believe that faith is a matter of merely subjective emotions, without a content to be known and a demand to be obeyed."[39] This distorts faith and religion in the same way as the strictly objective distortion and the existentialist interpretation by raising one element above all others. As Tillich says, "Certainly faith as an act of the whole personality has strong emotional elements within it."[40] But feeling may only play a role among other elements within a holistic understanding of faith as ultimate concern. Experience is not the source of faith; it is, rather, the medium through which the content of faith is accepted.[41]

Thinking about things pervades all of the spiritual activities of humanity, and humanity would not be spiritual without words,

---

36. See the editorial introduction to Tillich, *Dynamics of Faith*, 11.

37. Take note of Schleiermacher's implicit goals as expressed in *On Religion*, 26–29.

38. Tillich, *Reason and Revelation*, 42.

39. Tillich, *Dynamics of Faith*, 39.

40. Tillich, *Dynamics of Faith*, 40.

41. Tillich, *Reason and Revelation*, 42. Tillich would seemingly agree with Einstein, who reportedly once said, "Try and penetrate with our limited means the secrets of nature and you will find that, behind all the discernible laws and connections, there remains something subtle, intangible and inexplicable. Veneration for this force beyond anything that we can comprehend is my religion." Isaacson, "Einstein and Faith."

thoughts, and concepts.[42] This is especially true with regard to the concept of religion, the all-embracing function of a person's life. According to Tillich, it was Schleiermacher's error to define religion as "the feeling of ultimate dependence," and also a weakness of Schleiermacher's successors to locate religion in the realm of feelings. Indeed, for Tillich, the banishment of religion into a nonrational corner of subjective emotionality was a manner in which he (and others) escaped the conflict(s) of religion and modern thought. But, according to Tillich, this was a "death sentence" to religion, and fortunately religion did not accept it.[43] Tillich avers that religion objects to being turned into a synthesis of the spiritual functions, and it gives expression to this by refusing to admit a parity between the divine and the human, the holy and the natural spirit: it points to the radical difference between the holy and every cultural phenomenon.[44]

The essence of human consciousness is God-positing, an intellectual intuition of the identity between finite and absolute consciousness,[45] but at the same time it is estranged from its God-positing substantiality. Tillich agrees with Schelling that the essence of the religious picture is that "the formulation of a concept of religion must necessarily include a relationship between God and man that presupposes a definite division between them."[46] The problems besetting a satisfactory understanding of religion are increasingly evident. Yet religion itself continues and in many parts of the world appears perhaps to be resurgent. For a time some thought that the onslaught of science, comparative religion, uncertainty, and the rest—in a word, the onslaught of modernity—meant or would mean the gradual decline and disappearance of the religion; however, this no longer seems obvious.[47]

---

42. Tillich, *Reason and Revelation*, 15.

43. Tillich, *Reason and Revelation*, 15.

44. Tillich, "Philosophy of Religion," in *What Is Religion?*, 44.

45. Tillich, *Construction of the History*, 122.

46. Tillich, *Construction of the History*, 124.

47. Smith, *Meaning and End of Religion*, 9–10.

According to Smith, the concept of religion as we have inherited it today has been immensely enriched in content by the studies of the nineteenth century. He says that we, as heirs to the somewhat chaotic developments, commonly employ the term *religion* in four quite distinct senses. First, there is the sense of a personal piety; it is with this meaning that we use such phrases as, "He is more religious than he was ten years ago"; or if we remark that in every community that there are some people whose religion is harsh and narrow, others whose religion is warm and open.[48] Second and third, there is the usage that refers to an overt system, whether of beliefs, practices, values, or whatever; such a system has an extension of time, some relation to an area, and is related to a particular community—it is specific. In this sense, the word *religion* has a plural and in English the singular has an article. In each case, however, according to Smith, there are two contrasting meanings: one, of the system as an ideal, and the other, of it as an empirical phenomenon, both historical and sociological.[49] Thus there are two Christianities: "true Christianity" on the one hand, the ideal, which the theologian tries to formulate but which they know transcends them; and, on the other hand, the Christianity of history, which the sociologist or other observer notes as a human complex.

For example, Smith contends that normally persons talk about other people's religions as they are, and about their own as it ought to be, which is a basic reason why *religion* in the plural has maintained from the beginning a different meaning from the singular; in contrast, those without a faith of their own think of all *religions* as observably practiced; hence insiders and outsiders use the same words while talking of different things. Finally, there is *religion* as a generic summation, otherwise referred to as religion "in general"; the latter's meaning is inevitably derived for anyone using it, in part, from their sense of the other three—in so far as it is historical, it is as complex as all "the religions" taken together; in so far as it is personal, it is as diverse as the patron whose piety it synthesizes.[50] The

---

48. Smith, *Meaning and End of Religion*, 47.

49. Smith, *Meaning and End of Religion*, 47–48.

50. Smith, *Meaning and End of Religion*, 47–48.

proposal that Smith generates can, at one level, be formulated quite simply: what people have tended to conceive as religion can more truly be conceived in terms of two factors, different in kind, but nevertheless both dynamic: (1) an historical "cumulative tradition," and (2) the personal faith of men and women.[51] Smith proposes his pair of concepts—tradition and faith—to replace the currently established single one of "religion," without inquiring at length into the nature of the two. This is partly in line with Smith's concomitant thesis that the nature either of religious traditions or of faith is neither an intellectual desideratum nor a metaphysical reality; they are, rather, historical actualities, which must be explored as such.[52]

51. Smith, *Meaning and End of Religion*, 175.
52. Smith, *Meaning and End of Religion*, 176.

7

A Bridge to Faith

Tillich and Smith on Belief and Faith

THERE IS A BELIEF-FUL theoretical and practical behavior, but there is no belief-ful behavior as such, according to Tillich. Every act of faith is an embracing or shaping turn toward the Unconditional. Faith is neither mere *assensus*, nor mere *fiducia*; however, in every belief-ful *assensus* there is *fiducia*, and in every belief-ful *fiducia* there is *assensus*. "Unbelieffulness" is therefore the mark of the typically autonomous attitude of culture; but it is that only by intention. For Tillich, every creative cultural act is also belief-ful; in it pulsates the meaning of the Unconditional. Otherwise, it would in the end be without meaning and without import. But the cultural intention as an intention is unbelief-ful. It is that even when it is directed toward religious symbols; for it does not intend the Unconditional that shatters every symbol, but rather it intends the unity of the conditioned.[1]

In the Christian case, the matter has become complicated by the fact that in most Western languages the verb *credo*, "I believe," and so on, has come, since the eighteenth century or so, to be used both for intellectual belief and for religious faith—though persons of faith have tried to insist that "belief that" and "belief in"

---

1. Tillich, "Philosophy of Religion," in *What Is Religion?*, 76.

are two different matters.[2] Certainly true faith has already begun to crumble somewhat, if it has not actually gone, as soon as people have reduced what used to be the data, the presuppositions, of their worldview to a set of true or false propositions—when what was once the presupposed context for a transcending religious faith becomes rather the foreground of intellectual belief (true or false). This is one of the fundamental troubles in the modern world, and a fundamental problem arising from a recognition of religious diversity—that what used to be unconscious premises become, rather, scrutinized intellectualizations. At this new level, believers begin to wonder if they really "believe," in this new sense (and often enough find that actually they do not).[3]

For Tillich, all religious activity is cultic; religious activity, however, is belief-ful activity—thus, all belief-ful activity is therefore cultic.[4] This general concept of cultus is able to do justice to all forms of religious activity, and provides the clear parallel to the form of belief-ful cognition, i.e., to myth. In fact, the relation of myth and cultus is such that every cultic act has a mythical content, and every mythical object has a cultic realization; this complementarity of the two is based upon the faith character of both functions—for faith there can be no practical act that would not be directed toward the Unconditional through and beyond a symbol.[5] Faith belongs to a dimension other than any theoretical judgment. Faith is not belief and it is not knowledge with a low degree of probability; its certitude is not the uncertain certitude of a theoretical judgment.[6]

For Tillich, the truth of faith cannot be made dependent on the historical truth of the stories and legends in which faith has expressed itself, for example; it is a disastrous distortion of the meaning of faith to identify it with the belief in the historical validity of the biblical stories, therefore.[7] The Reformation emancipated

---

2. Smith, *Patterns of Faith*, 68–69.

3. Smith, *Patterns of Faith*, 69.

4. Tillich, "Philosophy of Religion," in *What Is Religion?*, 110.

5. Tillich, "Philosophy of Religion," in *What Is Religion?*, 110.

6. Tillich, *Dynamics of Faith*, 41.

7. Tillich, *Dynamics of Faith*, 84.

mankind from the law of action in late-Catholic heteronomy; but in accord with the spiritual situation it left the "law" of cognition untouched and inviolable. Modern Protestantism has freed mankind from the law of cognition, but has led into the emptiness of unbelief-ful autonomy. The meaning of a coming theonomy would be this: to be belief-ful in and through the autonomous form of knowledge and action.[8]

Faith is not simply an "act of knowledge that has a low degree of evidence";[9] this describes a belief, not faith. A belief is based upon evidence that is sufficient enough to add a high degree of probability. Indeed, a belief can be varied. We believe things when we have good evidence about them or when they are stated by good authorities. When we accept the authority's evidence as true it is often because we are unable to approach the evidence directly; history books are a good example of this—we are unable to prove that it happened because we weren't witness to it but believe it because we believe the author; this cannot be considered faith simply because although we trust the authorities, it is never unconditional; we do not have faith in them. Tillich states, "Faith is more than trust in authorities, although trust is an important element of faith."[10] Tillich uses this thought when he describes early biblical writers: Christians believe the writings but never unconditionally; they do not have faith in them and therefore "should not even have faith in the Bible."[11]

The most ordinary misinterpretation of faith, according to Tillich, is to consider it an act of knowledge that has a low degree of evidence. Something more or less probable or improbable is affirmed in spite of the insufficiency of its theoretical substantiation. This situation is very usual in daily life. If this is meant, one is speaking of belief rather than of faith. One believes that one's information is correct.[12] One believes that records of past events are

8. Tillich, "Philosophy of Religion," in *What Is Religion?*, 78.

9. Tillich, *Dynamics of Faith*, 36.

10. Tillich, *Dynamics of Faith*, 37.

11. Tillich, *Dynamics of Faith*, 37.

12. Tillich, *Dynamics of Faith*, 38.

useful for the reconstruction of facts.[13] One believes that a scientific theory is adequate for the understanding of a series of facts. One believes that a person will act in a specific way or that a political situation will change in a certain direction. In all these cases the belief is based on evidence sufficient to make the event probable. Sometimes, however, one believes something which has low probability or is strictly improbable, though not impossible. The causes for all these theoretical and practical beliefs are rather varied. Some things are believed because we have good though not complete evidence about them; many more things are believed because they are stated by good authorities. This is the case whenever we accept the evidence which others accepted as sufficient for belief, even if we cannot approach the evidence directly (for example, all events of the past). Here a new element comes into the picture, namely, the trust in the authority which makes a statement probable for us.

Without such trust we could not believe anything except the objects of our immediate experience. The consequence would be that our world would be infinitely smaller than it actually is. It is rational to trust in authorities which enlarge our consciousness without forcing us into submission. If we use the word *faith* for this kind of trust we can say that most of our knowledge is based on faith. But it is not appropriate to do so. We believe the authorities, we trust their judgment, though never unconditionally, but we do not have faith in them. Faith is more than trust in authorities, although trust is an element of faith. This distinction is important in view of the fact that some earlier theologians tried to prove the unconditional authority of the biblical writers by showing their trustworthiness as witnesses. The Christian may believe the biblical writers, but not unconditionally. He does not have faith in them. He should not even have faith in the Bible. For faith is more than trust in even the most sacred authority. It is participation in the subject of one's ultimate concern with one's whole being. Therefore, the term *faith* should not be used in connection with theoretical knowledge, whether it is a knowledge on the basis of immediate, prescientific or scientific

13. Tillich, *Dynamics of Faith*, 38–39.

evidence, or whether it is on the basis of trust in authorities who themselves are dependent on direct or indirect evidence.[14]

The terminological inquiry has led us into the material problem itself. Faith does not affirm or deny what belongs to the pre-scientific or scientific knowledge of our world, whether we know it by direct experience or through the experience of others. The knowledge of our world (including ourselves as a part of the world) is a matter of inquiry by ourselves or by those in whom we trust. It is not a matter of faith. The dimension of faith is not the dimension of science, history or psychology. The acceptance of a probable hypothesis in these realms is not faith, but preliminary belief, to be tested by scholarly methods and to be changed by every new discovery. Almost all the struggles between faith and knowledge are rooted in the wrong understanding of faith as a type of knowledge which has a low degree of evidence but is supported by religious authority. It is, however, not only confusion of faith with knowledge that is responsible for the world-historical conflicts between them; it is also the fact that matters of faith in the sense of ultimate concern lie hidden behind an assumedly scientific method. Whenever this happens, faith stands against faith and not against knowledge.

Unbelief, as Tillich defines it, is not the refusal or inability to give assent to certain theological doctrines but rather the expression of the fact that in his existential self-realization man "turns toward himself and his world and loses his essential unity with the ground of his being and his world."[15] Like its opposite, faith, it is an act of the total personality, involving knowledge, will, and emotion. This turning away from God and towards the self is expressed in various realms of human life. In the intellectual realm it is manifested in the disruption of man's cognitive participation in God. That this disruption occurs universally among men in the state of existence is evidenced by the fact that in this state men must ask for God. As Tillich puts it, "He who asks for God is already estranged from God, though not cut off from him."[16] In the moral realm, unbelief means

14. Tillich, *Dynamics of Faith*, 39.
15. Tillich, *Existence and the Christ*, 47.
16. Tillich, *Existence and the Christ*, 47.

the separation of the human from the divine will, and the universal occurrence of this separation is attested by the fact that men need a law which tells them how to act and which they can choose to obey or disobey; this shows that men are "already estranged from the source of the law which demands obedience."[17] In the realm of emotion, the universal occurrence of unbelief, or turning away from God, is manifested in the fact that humanity's love for self and its love for God are two distinct loves.[18] "In order to have a self which not only can be loved but can love God," Tillich declares, "one's center must already have left the divine center to which it belongs and in which self-love and love to God are united."[19]

The difference between faith and belief is also visible in the kind of certitude each gives. There are two types of knowledge which are based on complete evidence and give complete certitude. The one is the immediate evidence of sense perception; the other complete evidence is that of the logical and mathematical rules which are presupposed even if their formulation admits different and sometimes conflicting methods. According to Tillich, one of the worst errors of theology and popular religion is to make statements which intentionally or unintentionally contradict the structure of reality; such an attitude is not an expression of faith, but of the confusion of faith with belief.[20]

In Tillich's view, faith is not a belief that something has a certain degree of probability. Faith is not a type of theoretical knowledge that is based on probability. Tillich says that many historical conflicts have resulted from the misunderstanding of faith as a type of knowledge supported by religious authority. Faith is not an act of knowledge related to uncertainty, explains Tillich, nor is it a belief based on incomplete evidence. Because it is not an act of knowledge, faith does not have to be supplemented by an act of will. Thus, the will to believe does not create faith. In discussing the truth of faith, Tillich examines the relation between faith and reason. Faith is not

17. Tillich, *Existence and the Christ*, 47.
18. Martin, *Existentialist Theology of Paul Tillich*, 120–21.
19. Tillich, *Existence and the Christ*, 48.
20. Tillich, *Dynamics of Faith*, 41.

in conflict with reason. Tillich says that reason is a precondition for faith, and that faith is an act in which reason ecstatically transcends itself. Ecstasy does not deny rationality, but fulfills it. Reason fulfills itself when it brings an awareness of the presence of ultimate reality.

In Tillich's view, faith is not a belief that something has a certain degree of probability. Faith is not a type of theoretical knowledge that is based on probability. Tillich says that many historical conflicts have resulted from the misunderstanding of faith as a type of knowledge supported by religious authority. Faith is not an act of knowledge related to uncertainty, explains Tillich, nor is it a belief based on incomplete evidence. Because it is not an act of knowledge, it does not have to be supplemented by an act of will. Thus, the will to believe does not create faith. In discussing the truth of faith, Tillich examines the relation between faith and reason. Faith is not in conflict with reason. Tillich claims that reason is a precondition for faith, and that faith is an act in which reason ecstatically transcends itself. Ecstasy does not deny rationality, but fulfills it. Reason fulfills itself when it brings an awareness of the presence of ultimate reality.

Smith spent much of his career persuading people that faith and belief should never be confused with each other, drawing on his vast knowledge of history of religions and comparative cultural history to make his point.[21] Smith has argued that while objective empirical evidence and corroboration are necessary for meaningfulness of a religious statement, it is not sufficient unless there is confirmation also by the subjective testimony of the insider or member of the respective faith. An integral part of faith, Smith asserts, is a personal response to that proposition or experience. Faith implies engagement, interaction, while belief involves only an intellectual assertion that something may be true and correct.[22] If "faith" for Smith is the "integration of a coherent personal life with the universe around us, a universe seen as endowed with coherence and order," and a personal praxis at that, then, even at the risk of a

---

21. Cox, "Faith and Belief Revisited," 112.
22. Smith, *Faith and Belief*, 4–5, 50.

mild apologia, the Vedic religious orientation ought to go through as a specimen of faith.[23]

For Smith, a "belief," with its naturalistic bias, has a certain structure (i.e., propositional) and lends itself to cognitive and rational affirmation or disaffirmation, and is open to semantic and syntactical scrutiny as well as doubt; or it may remain neutral as to its correctness.[24] Faith has none of these properties, or those requiring its "work" or function to be judged by the same parameters and naturalistic criteria that apply to belief.[25] Consider Gettier's strict requirement of epistemological and logical strictures of justified true belief:[26] a belief is nothing if it cannot be justified with empirical observations and collaborative evidence; even then, it might fail because the supposed conclusion—the belief—might be derived equally naturally from two counterfactually conflicting premises; it doesn't matter in analytical dissection whether the whole holds together against the grain of the dissipating and fragmentary parts[27] (and the fragmentation under the ruse of deconstruction or "tearing" is taken to its logical conclusion in postmodernism).[28] Such an outcome would have the inwardly felt truths of religion subjected to the rigors and limitations of logic that might never allow the subjective, phenomenological dimension of religion to emerge and survive.

In *Believing: An Historical Perspective*,[29] Smith addresses how, why, and with what implications our understanding of the terms *faith* and *belief* has altered with time. Is what, or whether, one believes the significant religious question? Although the religious communities differ in belief, how much do they really differ in faith? Do two people who assert a particular statement of belief necessarily share the same faith? The English word *belief*, Smith

23. Bilmoria, "Meaningful 'End' of God," 80.
24. Smith, *Faith and Belief*, 35.
25. Smith, *Faith and Belief*, 35.
26. Bilmoria, "Meaningful 'End' of God," 78.
27. Bilmoria, "Meaningful 'End' of God," 78.
28. See Taylor, *After God*.
29. Smith, *Believing*, 61.

asserts, is no longer an adequate translation of the concept of those who wrote the original text.[30] Smith suggests that there are three modern usages of *belief.*

First, it may be used in the sense of a person reporting that another recognizes a particular fact. Second, it may imply that one is of the opinion that a particular fact is the case. Third, it may mean that one imagines a particular fact to be true.[31] The differences between these three meanings are subtle, but nevertheless important: in the first instance—the recognition of a fact—both those reporting and those believing are certain that the fact in question is correct; by contrast, the second possibility—an opinion about the veracity of a fact—implies that there is a large measure of doubt on the part of the person reporting the fact and possibly also on the part of the person said to hold that opinion; the third possibility—i.e., of imagining a fact—implies that the person reporting the belief is sure that it is incorrect, fanciful even. Smith contends that belief was once used to imply recognition, but has come to imply opinion or even an imagining. To suggest that the Bible's authors hoped people would come to hold a certain opinion about God makes a mockery of them. Instead, they hoped people would recognize the truth they had also seen, and that this would have an existential impact upon people's lives.

The (post-)modern meaning of *belief* as opinion, Smith contends, has no place in an honest translation of the Bible, possibly with the single exception of the "belief" of demons in God found in the letter of James.[32] For most of history, the words "I believe" have been essentially a declaration of faith, but of belief only in very general, overarching terms. Indeed, "I believe" once meant more of the commitment and engagement of the individual who uttered the phrase than of the specifics of what was or was not believed. In general, however, today, phrases such as "he believes" or "they believe" are more common than the phrase "I believe" and indicate a particular set of specific facts believed in (or perceived to

30. Smith, *Believing,* 53.

31. Smith, *Believing,* 58.

32. Smith, *Believing,* 79.

be believed in) by the individuals who are the subject of the comment. "I believe" still usually indicates that what follows is not so much a list of specific facts, but a declaration of commitment to and engagement with a particular tradition (or, conceivably, an amalgamation of several traditions). Smith backs up my contention that a creed is not a list of propositions we have to assent to but is a badge of *belonging* instead. As such, one does not have to make a mental effort to say they believe in the list of doctrines contained in the creed; rather one says they commit themselves to a journey of faith, using the Christian story as their symbolic guideposts.

Smith notes that for many people in the contemporary era, *belief* conjures up a notion of holding certain ideas, agreeing with some proposition (such as that there is a God). This confusion, between having faith and believing, was one of the major grounds for Smith's hesitation about retaining the word *faith* in the title of his book, *Patterns of Faith Around the World* (1962). He contends that simply to be a theist is by no means to be a person of faith, whereas to be a nontheist is by no means not to have faith. Furthermore, belief is not faith; it is one expression of faith, at a conceptual and verbal level. Believing something, as an intellectual stance, is at a considerably lower level than the deeply personal one, of living in, and by, faith. ("Oh ye of little faith" was not addressed to those whose ideology was deficient.) Many have, in the contemporary context, according to Smith, rejected the word, and what they think of as its meaning; his retaining the word *faith* is because he has something quite else in mind.[33]

According to Smith, faith differs from belief in many ways, and goes beyond it; one way is that faith in God's oneness is a recognition of his unique and exclusive authority, and an active giving of oneself to it.[34] The Christian and classical Muslim, both, would understand at once James in the New Testament writing, "You believe that God is one? You do well: the devils also recognize [Smith says that "believe" here is a mistranslation] and tremble."[35]

33. Smith, *Patterns of Faith*, 13.

34. Smith, *Patterns of Faith*, 69.

35. Smith, *Patterns of Faith*, 69. Smith's translation of Jas 2:19 is from the King James Authorized and Revised Standard versions of the Bible. Smith,

To a truly religious person, the question is not one merely of seeing the facts—let alone merely of believing this or that—but of doing something about it.[36]

Smith's text entitled *Faith and Belief: The Difference Between Them*,[37] gives an overview of the growth and development of his original thesis, presented in *The Meaning and End of Religion*, which he still holds to be valid. It represents an orientation best summed up in his oft repeated "The study of religion is the study of persons." There are two intertwined themes in Smith's *Faith and Belief*. One is historical: this is that in the early centuries the *faith* which the Church sought of those to baptized was not "belief that" certain propositions were true, but a *commitment*, a *pledging of allegiance* to God in Christ.[38] Smith also holds that the *faith* which the Bible commends is *commitment* rather than *belief* in the contemporary sense of the term; but he does not argue that here, as that was a theme of his companion volumes, *Belief and History* and *Believing: A Historical Perspective*.

Even the English word *believe* in the late Middle Ages used to mean "to hold dear" or "to value highly."[39] The difference between the "believer" and the "non believer" was not that they had different views about the world but that the believer had an allegiance to God which the non believer lacked. In recent centuries, however, Smith argues, there has been a change in the meaning of *believe* without there being any change in the wording of creedal and similar formulae. In consequence, what the Christian church now seeks of its members is belief that certain propositions are true and, less so, thereby, *dedication* and *commitment* to God. Yet it has become difficult for modern humanity to believe the propositions in question, which reflect bygone worldview. Some have forced themselves to "believe," but at the cost of intellectual honesty. Others who were potentially people of faith have been driven away from the church by

---

Patterns of Faith, 153n17.

36. Smith, *Patterns of Faith*, 69.
37. Smith, *Faith and Belief*, 3–69.
38. Smith, *Faith and Belief*, viii.
39. Smith, *Faith and Belief*, 73.

the requirement of "belief." What is important for religion, according to Smith, is commitment to and love of a transcendent reality, not the particular set of theses in terms of which about the transcendent is conceptualized, and above all not humanity's *beliefs* (in the (post-)modern sense) about these matters.[40] Smith asserts that faith is one, although differently expressed.

40. Smith, *Faith and Belief*, 141.

8

The Key to All Things

Tillich and Smith on Faith Alone

In his introduction to *Dynamics of Faith*, Paul Tillich states, "There is hardly a word in the religious language, both theological and popular, which is subject to more misunderstandings, distortions,[1] and questionable definitions than the word 'faith.'"[2] In probably his most widely read work, *The Courage to Be*, Tillich reinterprets the idea of faith, both to correct misconceptions and to enable readers to experience the underlying power and meaning of faith. Because he grounds faith ontologically and existentially, his analysis of faith connects to all functions of human spiritual life and to everyday living. His existential analysis includes psychological aspects of faith and recognizes great diversity in the contents of people's faith, as well as destructive and sometimes pathological forms of faith. Moreover, Tillich's theological understanding of faith and his critique of forms and contents of faith, while rooted in Christian tradition, extends outside Christianity to include other religions and even secular forms of faith.

Tillich notes that every theologian is both committed and alienated at the same time: he is always in both faith and doubt, for

1. Tillich, *Dynamics of Faith*, 1.
2. Tillich, *Dynamics of Faith*, ix.

he is inside and outside—simultaneously—the "theological circle."[3] Tillich claims that at one point one side prevails, and at another the other side prevails, and one can never be sure which side ultimately will prevail. So then, a person can be a theologian only if he acknowledges the content of his theological circle as his "ultimate concern."[4] Whether this is true or not, does *not* depend on one's intellectual or moral certitude of faith or belief, but upon one's being ultimately concerned with the content of his belief and faith instead.[5] Indeed, "Our ultimate concern can destroy us as it can heal us. But we can never be without it."[6]

Tillich states that faith is both conscious and unconscious; indeed, since faith is the total act of personality, it is impossible to imagine faith without the unconscious elements of one's personality. Tillich defines faith as being in a state of ultimate concern or loving something with all our mind, body, and spirit. Examples of an object of our ultimate concern include money, God, our materiality, etc. The object of our ultimate concern becomes our god. Tillich averred that the essence of religious attitudes is "ultimate concern." Ultimate concern is "total" and totalizing—its object is experienced as numinous or holy, distinct from the profane and ordinary realities. Tillich asserts that faith is a task for the believer's complete being—it is an act of both the conscious and the unconscious. God, says Tillich, is present as the subject and object of ultimate faith while at the same time is transcendent beyond both subject and object.

In 1957, Tillich defined his conception of faith more explicitly in his work *Dynamics of Faith*. He notes that, "Man, like every living being, is concerned about many things, above all about those which condition his very existence. . . . If [a situation or concern] claims ultimacy it demands the total surrender of him who accepts this claim. . . . It demands that all other concerns . . . be sacrificed."[7]

3. Tillich, *Reason and Revelation*, 10.

4. Tillich, *Reason and Revelation*, 10.

5. Tillich, *Reason and Revelation*, 10.

6. Tillich, *Dynamics of Faith*, 18.

7. Tillich, *Dynamics of Faith*, 1–2.

Tillich further states that, "Faith as ultimate concern is an act of the total personality. It is the most centered act of the human mind. . . . It participates in the dynamics of personal life."[8]

For Tillich, faith is the state of being ultimately concerned: it demands total surrender to the subject of *ultimate concern*. Faith is more than the sum of its parts, however, as it has a transcendent quality. It is more than religion, more than believing, more than acting, more than understanding; these verbs are elements of faith, but faith goes beyond all of them. Faith is ecstatic—it allows a person to stand outside of herself without ceasing to be herself. It is both the belief itself and the thing that makes that belief possible. Faith is constitutive of relationships. In order for a person to be in relationship with another being, there must be both subject and object. True faith focuses on God (that which is truly ultimate) as its ultimate concern, and so subject and object become one. Tillich refers to God as "being-itself," and as such, God is at the center of each human existence. Faith connects our essential being to God's essential being (being-itself), and transcends all human experience. Tillich notes that "Reason is the precondition of faith; faith is the act in which reason reaches ecstatically beyond itself."[9] Indeed, according to Tillich, "Faith cannot guarantee factual truth. But faith can and must interpret the meaning of facts from the point of view of man's ultimate concern."[10] Tillich contends, further, "Faith stands upon itself and justifies itself against those who attack it, because they can attack it only in the name of another faith. It is the triumph of the dynamics of faith that any denial of faith is itself an expression of faith, of an ultimate concern."[11]

"Faith can give certainty," Tillich writes, "only to the victory of the Christ over the ultimate consequence of the existential estrangement to which he subjected himself."[12] This certainty of faith is immediate because faith itself rests upon it. In the experience

8. Tillich, *Dynamics of Faith*, 5.
9. Tillich, *Dynamics of Faith*, 87.
10. Tillich, *Dynamics of Faith*, 99.
11. Tillich, *Dynamics of Faith*, 147.
12. Tillich, *Existence and the Christ*, 159.

of being grasped by the power of the new being as manifested in Jesus as the Christ, the experience which—according to Tillich—is faith, one is certain of "one's own victory over the death of existential estrangement" and this certainty.[13] The characteristics of the regenerated state are the opposite of those of the state of estrangement—faith instead of unbelief, surrender instead of *hubris*, love instead of concupiscence.[14]

The certitude of faith is existential, meaning that the whole existence of man is involved; as such, it has two elements: the one, which is not a risk but a certainty about one's own being, namely, on being related to something ultimate or unconditional; the other, which is a risk and involves doubt and courage insomuch as the surrender to a concern which is not really ultimate and may be destructive if taken as ultimate. This destructive possibility is not a theoretical problem of the kind of higher or lower evidence, of probability or improbability, but it is an existential problem of "to be or not to be" (so to speak). It belongs to a dimension other than any theoretical judgment. Faith is not belief and it is not knowledge with a low degree of probability. Its certitude is not the uncertain certitude of a theoretical judgment.[15]

Directedness toward the Unconditional, of which we have spoken in connection with the derivation of the concept of the nature of religion, Tillich calls faith.[16] In fact, "faith is a turning toward the Unconditional, effective in all functions of the spirit. . . . Faith, therefore, is not identical with any one of the other functions, neither with the theoretical, as a frequent misunderstanding supposes, nor with the practical, as the opposing conception contends."[17] In consequence, faith is not the acceptance of uncertain objects as true; in fact, it has nothing to do with acceptance or probability. Neither is it merely the establishing of a community relationship, like confidence or obedience or the like; rather, "it is the apprehension of the Unconditional

---

13. Martin, *Existentialist Theology of Paul Tillich*, 166.

14. Martin, *Existentialist Theology of Paul Tillich*, 170.

15. Tillich, *Dynamics of Faith*, 41.

16. Tillich, "Philosophy of Religion," in *What Is Religion?*, 75.

17. Tillich, "Philosophy of Religion," in *What Is Religion?*, 75.

as the ground of both the theoretical and the practical."[18] However, faith is also no special function alongside other functions; rather, it comes to expression only in them, as their root. God is the object intended in faith, and beyond that nothing.[19] This, however, is not to say that the object is, as it were, to be made into a product of the subject, as though God were a creation of faith.

Faith in God is the basis for a courage which conquers the negativities of the temporal process. Neither the anxiety of the past nor that of the future remains. The anxiety of the past is conquered by the freedom of God toward the past and its potentialities. The anxiety of the future is conquered by the dependence of the new on the unity of the divine life.[20] The dissected moments of time are united in eternity. Here, and not in a doctrine of the human soul, is rooted the certainty of man's participation in eternal life. The hope of eternal life is based not on a substantial quality of mankind's soul but on his participation in the eternity of the divine life.[21]

Omnipresence symbolizes God's relation to space. Omnipresence is, for Tillich, the symbol for God's "creative participation in the spatial existence of his creatures."[22] But God's participation in extension or spatiality does not mean his subjection to it.[23] Participating in spatial existence, God nevertheless transcends it; it is faith in the omnipresent God, Tillich concludes,[24] which gives humanity the courage to overcome the anxiety of not having a permanent place that is his own and to accept the contingencies of his spatial existence.[25]

Faith also includes uncertainty and doubt: doubt is not lack of faith, but rather is a necessary element to true faith. As humans, we are finite beings. We must accept our finitude, and we must accept

18. Tillich, "Philosophy of Religion," in *What Is Religion?*, 75.

19. Tillich, "Philosophy of Religion," in *What Is Religion?*, 79.

20. Martin, *Existentialist Theology of Paul Tillich*, 153.

21. Tillich, *Existence and the Christ*, 61.

22. Tillich, *Existence and the Christ*, 86–89.

23. Tillich, *Existence and the Christ*, 62.

24. Tillich, *Existence and the Christ*, 63.

25. Martin, *Existentialist Theology of Paul Tillich*, 153–54.

an element of uncertainty in our faith. The element of faith which accepts this uncertainty is courage, upon which Tillich has written an entire book (*The Courage to Be*)—but I will quote his summary of the concept in that "courage as an element of faith is the daring self-affirmation of one's own being in spite of the powers of 'non-being' which are the heritage of everything finite."[26] According to Tillich, doubt is a necessary consequence of the risk of faith, and it must be experienced and accepted through courage. Doubt is not a permanent experience, but it is always present as one element in the structure of faith; it is, then, in faith in God symbolized as omnipotent creator that Tillich, in his *Systematic Theology*, finds the source of a person's courage to be and to overcome the anxiety of nonbeing. The content of this faith cannot be given to man by any resources of his own, but is "spoken" to human existence from beyond it, according to Tillich.[27] The existential experience of revelation alone has produced the classical symbols in which Christianity has expressed its experience of God.[28] Courage in faith does not repress doubt but includes it as an awareness of the risk of faith, the element of "in spite of," taking seriously the experience of doubt.[29]

The doubt which is implicit in faith is not a doubt about facts or conclusions; as such, it is not the same doubt which is the lifeblood of scientific research.[30] There is another kind of doubt, which Tillich calls skeptical, in contrast to the scientific doubt, which he calls methodological. The skeptical doubt is an attitude toward all the beliefs of man, from sense experiences to religious creeds. It is more an attitude than an assertion, for as an assertion it would conflict with itself. Even the assertion that there is no possible truth for humanity would be judged by the skeptical principle and could not stand as an assertion. Genuine skeptical doubt does not use the form of an assertion; it is an attitude of actually rejecting any certainty.

26. Tillich, *Courage to Be*, 19.

27. Tillich, *Existence and the Christ*, 67.

28. Martin, *Existentialist Theology of Paul Tillich*, 156–57.

29. Stenger, "Faith (and Religion)," 95–96.

30. Tillich, *Dynamics of Faith*, 28.

Therefore, it cannot be refuted logically.[31] Doubt, for Tillich, is a reflection—or more specifically, a recognition—that one's ultimate concern is in fact *ultimate*. Tillich notes, "If doubt appears, it should not be considered as the negation of faith, but as an element which was always and will always be present in the act of faith. Existential doubt and faith are poles of the same reality, the state of ultimate concern. But serious doubt is confirmation of faith, as it indicates the seriousness of the concern, its unconditional character."[32]

Discussion of faith for Tillich includes ontological, existential and psychological aspects, with these connecting further to epistemological and ethical dimensions.[33] "Faith is the state of being ultimately concerned," Tillich asserts.[34] This formal definition of faith focuses on a person's state of being (ontological), his or her individual connection to ultimacy (ontological, existential and psychological) and the experience of concern (subjective: existential and psychological). "Faith as ultimate concern is an act of the total personality," Tillich argues, providing an understanding so much deeper, broader and more existentially significant than the view of faith as belief, especially when that belief is understood to have a low degree of evidence.[35] Nor is faith acceptance of creeds or church practices and authorities, although people may find their existential experience of faith confirmed and celebrated in such creeds and institutional authorities.[36]

Tillich's ontological analysis focuses on persons of faith experiencing their ontological connection to ultimacy (power of being, ground of being, being-itself, God), a connection he sees as universal.[37] He describes this experience as "the state of being grasped by the power of being-itself," offering that description as a definition

31. Tillich, *Dynamics of Faith*, 29.
32. Tillich, *Dynamics of Faith*, 31.
33. Stenger, "Faith (and Religion)," 91.
34. Tillich, *Dynamics of Faith*, 1.
35. Tillich, *Dynamics of Faith*, 1; Tillich, *Existence and the Christ*, 47.
36. Tillich, *Existence and the Christ*, 85.
37. Stenger, "Faith (and Religion)," 91–92.

of faith (as well as of religion).[38] The power of being-itself is present in people's everyday life experiences of affirming being and life in the face of threats of nonbeing, such as death, doubt, and guilt. For Tillich, everyone participates in the power of being and the power of being in them.[39] That participation is the ontological ground of faith, the ontological basis for "being grasped by the power of being which transcends everything that is and in which everything that is participates."[40] People may not consciously recognize this presence, but when they do, they are experiencing faith. With his understanding of faith as ultimate concern, Tillich emphasizes that all people experience something as ultimate that engenders their commitment (even if that something is not ultimate in truth).[41]

The source of this experience is the human "awareness of the infinite" to which all humans belong. This is not just a casual awareness but involves participation, Tillich emphasizes: "There is no faith without participation!"[42] Tillich speaks of humans as "driven toward faith" by this awareness of the infinite to which we belong.[43] That connection to the infinite or ultimate is the basis of the courage to face the challenges of everyday life. This ontological, existential understanding of faith connects to Tillich's psychological analysis of faith. Tillich argues that faith includes both the unconscious and conscious elements in the personality. If faith were only an unconscious act, it would be a compulsion. But faith is free, even though faith can involve unconscious strivings that affect the type of faith and choice of symbols to which a person responds.[44] On the conscious level, faith as one's ultimate commitment provides a uniting center that influences and even regulates daily life. Faith deepens every aspect of one's life, including artistic creativity,

38. Tillich, *Courage to Be*, 172.

39. Stenger, "Faith (and Religion)," 92.

40. Tillich, *Courage to Be*, 173.

41. Stenger, "Faith (and Religion)," 92.

42. Tillich, *Dynamics of Faith*, 100.

43. Tillich, *Dynamics of Faith*, 9.

44. Stenger, "Faith (and Religion)," 92–93.

scientific knowing, forming of ethics, organizing of politics, setting of personal discipline, and contemplation.[45]

Although Tillich's ontological analysis of faith emphasizes the integrating, positive qualities of it, he is well aware of the distortions of faith, both in the understandings of what faith is and in the contents of faith. On the subjective side, faith is the experience of ultimacy, but one must evaluate whether that experience is holistic and integrated or partial and perhaps pathological and destructive.[46] On the objective side of faith is the element of ultimacy itself, where distortions involve the content of what one holds as ultimate.[47] Holding as ultimate that which is not ultimate (idolatry) can be existentially disappointing, disrupting, and destructive.[48] For Tillich, there are many degrees in the endless realm of false ultimacies. According to him, the more idolatrous a faith the less it is able to overcome the cleavage between subject and object. Humans frequently substitute other things for God as the content of their ultimate concern, and thereby in their individual acts of faith. Everyone has an ultimate concern, for that is part of what it means to be human, for Tillich at least.

Distortions on the subjective side relate to epistemology and psychology. A common misrepresentation of faith is to see it as belief with little evidence or as trust in authorities. But such acceptance and trust in authorities is not *faith* by Tillich's definition; rather, that trust and acceptance are part of the broader process of humans seeking, testing, and judging knowledge about themselves and their world.[49] Such knowledge has varying degrees of probability, ranging from the certainty of empirical experience and mathematical rules to claims far removed from empirical observation.[50] But faith as ultimate concern is not subject to verification or disproving through varying degrees of evidence; because faith involves

---

45. Tillich, *Dynamics of Faith*, 107.
46. Stenger, "Faith (and Religion)," 93.
47. Stenger, "Faith (and Religion)," 94.
48. Tillich, *Dynamics of Faith*, 12.
49. Tillich, *Dynamics of Faith*, 31–33.
50. Stenger, "Faith (and Religion)," 94.

the whole human personality, the certainty of faith is "existential."[51] One can center one's faith in something less than ultimate, leading to existential disappointment and destructive results. Tillich sees this on a deeper level than experiences of certainty or uncertainty with respect to empirical or theoretical judgments. Psychological distortions of faith include focus on the will (voluntarist) or focus on the emotions.[52]

The misrepresentation of faith as the will to believe connects to understanding faith as belief with little evidence. If there is insufficient evidence to compel belief, then an act of faith must be an act of the will over against one's normal doubt or questioning. Even if one understands this act of the will as given by God's grace, the context for so moving one's will is usually a structure of authority. Over against such a view, Tillich argues that faith as ultimate concern is primary, with obedience stemming from the commitment of one's ultimate concern rather than the will enacting or originating the faith. "No command to believe and no will to believe can create faith."[53]

On the objective side of faith, it is the ultimate that is given specific content in people's particular forms of faith and in different types of courage. Faith has a content towards which people direct their commitments and ultimate concern. Many contents of faith can be false ultimacies or forms of idolatry, elevating a finite preliminary reality to ultimacy.[54] Idolatrous faith is still faith, still ultimate concern experienced as free, ecstatic, and promising fulfilment, but Tillich argues that idolatrous faith will disappoint a person existentially, disrupting rather than centering and uniting the personality.[55] Both sides of faith—the subjective and the objective—are subject to distortion, sometimes with disastrous consequences for individuals (or occasionally, even for groups).

---

51. Tillich, *Dynamics of Faith*, 34.
52. Stenger, "Faith (and Religion)," 94.
53. Tillich, *Dynamics of Faith*, 38.
54. Tillich, *Dynamics of Faith*, 11–12.
55. Tillich, *Dynamics of Faith*, 12.

Faith, then, involves a risk—a risk that the content of faith is not truly ultimate (idolatry) or even that what one affirms as real is not real (neurosis).[56] But such risk does not and cannot keep people from faith, although the risks can lead people to deep questioning of traditional contents and even forms of faith. Because Tillich's analysis is open to secular as well as traditionally religious contents, deep questioning may lead to different forms of faith but, in his view, not to a state of no faith.[57] For Tillich, faith involves a more fundamental risk: doubt. "Courage does not deny that there is doubt, but it takes the doubt into itself as an expression of its own finitude and affirms the content of an ultimate concern."[58]

Persons and communities of faith have regularly recognized that therein they are in touch with something, *someone*, beyond the ordinary world; something within them, around them, yet "above" them, greater than they; it exceeds their grasp, but not their reach; their comprehension, but not their apprehension.[59] This Smith calls "transcendence." Smith points out that one notable feature within the history of faith is that those involved have tended to assert that their faith derives from a transcendent source, even constitutes a human relationship with a transcendent reality.[60] The negative side, for Smith, of this has underlain the attitude of some religious groups or persons that their view of the universe is absolute, indisputably right, and that any position that differs is therefore indisputably wrong and to be dismissed, if not to be crushed.

Countering this, one may accept the premise but draw rather the inference that we have here been at pains to stress: that any human apprehension in the faith realm is inevitably partial, usually markedly partial and inadequate, and sometimes downright destructive; the claim of a relationship to a transcendent source deserves to be taken seriously.[61] For Smith, faith is the search for

---

56. Stenger, "Faith (and Religion)," 94–95.
57. Stenger, "Faith (and Religion)," 95.
58. Tillich, *Courage to Be*, 101.
59. Smith, *Patterns of Faith*, 13–14.
60. Smith, *Patterns of Faith*, 14.
61. Smith, *Patterns of Faith*, 14.

conceptual clarification of humanity's relation to transcendence. To speak more concretely, many persons in modern times have found that there is less difference between the faith of Christians and that of Muslims and of Hindus than is among the formulae and symbols by which that faith is visibly stressed. Secondly, they have found that the faith of a particular Christian may, once the outward wrappings are set aside, differ from the faith a Muslim or a Hindu less than it differs from the faith of another Christian next door or in a different denomination or a different century.

For Smith, personal faith differs from person to person and from day to day, in depth and genuineness, in force and vividness, in expression. Yet it is a thesis of his *Patterns of Faith Around the World* (1962) that basically it is and has been more humanly universal than any of these variegated forms in which it finds outward expression. Faith, then, like courage, like humility or pride, like love, truth, fear, cannot be observed directly. These cannot be investigated "objectively"—none of them is an object in the world; they are qualities in persons' hearts and minds. They can be suggested, by examples of occasions when, and forms through which, they have found human manifestation. Sensitive observers can and regularly do move from observing the outward signs towards learning and appreciating the human quality involved in a particular case—though further occasions may provide new insights.[62] Thus, faith is indefinable, Smith affirms.[63]

According to Smith, faith can only be suggested; that is, inferred only. It can be finitely evinced—in various forms, including conceptually. Involved here is a sense of that transcendent reality to which faith has been said to be a relation, as well as the source from which it derives. The very fact of its being the human awareness of and response to that reality, and the very fact of that reality's being transcendent, together explain, and even entail, the further fact of inescapable limitation of any instances of faith here on earth. How then could faith be defined? Smith's view is that any appreciation of beauty; any striving for truth; any pursuit of justice; any recognition

---

62. Smith, *Patterns of Faith*, 12.
63. Smith, *Patterns of Faith*, 14–15.

that some things are good, some are bad, and that it matters; any feeling or practice of love; any love of what theists call "God"; all these and more are examples of personal, and communal, faith.[64] The element of doubt in faith is balanced by the experience of "immediate certainty" in faith that stems from the Unconditional itself, that grounds one's ultimate concern. That experience of the Unconditional always connects to concrete content that can be doubted, asking whether the content is truly ultimate.[65] The possibility of idolatry exists, as people can easily take something finite as ultimate or use the bearer of the ultimate for finite purposes, a possibility that Tillich counters with the criterion against idolatry: the cross of the Christ.[66] But not only does the cross critique any absolutizing of the finite, it also affirms God's connection to humans. God acts and gives in faith, rather than humans giving to God; Tillich calls this "the only absolute content of faith, namely, that in relation to the ultimate we are always receiving and never giving."[67]

Tillich distinguishes two basic types of faith that are interdependent and rooted in human experiences of ultimacy or "the holy."[68] In ontological faith, the experience of the presence of the holy breaking into ordinary reality, the experience of the "holiness of being" dominates. In the moral type of faith, a person is more aware of the judgment of the holy over everything, experiencing the "holiness of what ought to be" as predominant. Within the ontological type of faith Tillich includes sacramental faith, where one experiences something as holy, i.e., where one is grasped by holiness through the medium of something concrete.[69] In contrast, mystical faith emphasizes the finite quality of all concrete forms and encourages experience beyond concreteness in the "abyss of pure divinity." This experience of faith turns inward to the "depth of the human soul," to the "point" of encounter of finite and infinite, a

---

64. Smith, *Patterns of Faith*, 14–15.

65. Tillich, *Dynamics of Faith*, 102–4.

66. Tillich, *Dynamics of Faith*, 97, 104.

67. Tillich, *Dynamics of Faith*, 105.

68. Tillich, *Dynamics of Faith*, 56.

69. See Tillich, *Dynamics of Faith*, 58.

point of emptiness of all concrete forms and preliminary concerns, to a depth that goes beyond subject and object, to a point where the ultimate overcomes that duality.[70]

Yet another form of ontological faith does not transcend humanity or the human world, instead focusing on the ideals of humanity. Humanism is an ontological, secular form of faith, experiencing ultimacy in ideals or essential qualities of humanity that move beyond the distortions of our actual world but are seen as possible within the human world.[71] Shifting to the moral types of faith, Tillich distinguishes juristic, conventional, and ethical types in a discussion that tends towards stereotyping the approaches of non-Christian faith traditions; he identifies Talmudic Judaism and Islam as following juristic approaches, Confucian China as conventional, and Jewish prophetic faith as ethical.[72] Although these types of faith may reflect ontological forms, such as the mystical or sacramental, in Tillich's view they emphasize analysis of laws and obedience because the laws express "what ought to be," experienced in Judaism and Islam both as God's gift and God's command.[73]

In analyzing the truth of faith, Tillich distinguishes truth on the subjective side of faith and truth on the objective side of faith. Subjectively, faith is true for someone if it "adequately expresses an ultimate concern." Objectively, "faith is true if its content is the really ultimate." For a symbol adequately to express an ultimate concern, it must create "reply, action, communication."[74] Symbols both live and die, expressing thereby a group's ultimate concern for a time but then becoming inadequate and part of the history of the group. So subjectively, faith is true if it is alive for people, if it works, if it evokes a response in them. The history of faith traditions focuses on this subjective side, expressing what people have found to be an adequate expression of their ultimate concern. The more

---

70. See Tillich, *Dynamics of Faith*, 60–61.

71. See Tillich, *Dynamics of Faith*, 63.

72. Stenger, "Faith (and Religion)," 98.

73. Tillich, *Dynamics of Faith*, 65–66.

74. Tillich, *Dynamics of Faith*, 96.

challenging test of faith addresses the objective side.[75] In *Dynamics of Faith*, Tillich uses the symbol of the cross as the criterion of the truth of faith on the content, or objective, side. The cross of the Christ expresses Jesus' self-sacrifice that simultaneously affirms and negates Jesus as the Christ. The criterion of the truth of faith, then, is self-negation, that the ultimate itself can be manifest but no human or finite thing can hold that ultimacy. "That symbol is most adequate which expresses not only the ultimate but also its own lack of ultimacy."[76] Thus, faith holds the tension of doubt and risk, and faith requires courage.[77]

75. Stenger, "Faith (and Religion)," 101.

76. Tillich, *Dynamics of Faith*, 97.

77. Stenger, "Faith (and Religion)," 101.

Conclusion

The Meaning and End of *Religio*—
The Ultimate Concern

THROUGH AN ETYMOLOGICAL STUDY of "religion" (*religio*, in Latin), Smith[1] contends that the term, which at first (as well as for most of the centuries in antiquity) denoted an attitude towards a relationship between God and "man"[2] (*sic*) has, through conceptual slippage, come to mean a "system of observances or beliefs,"[3]

1. In 1984, Whaling hinted at eight concepts potentially embodying the legacy of Smith: (1) His stress upon persons; (2) His concern to understand the worldview of others; (3) His notion that religious truth must encompass the data of faith as well as the data of the ongoing tradition; (4) His global awareness of the total human community; (5) His perception that the Transcendent Reality (however defined) is part of the subject matter of the study of religion; (6) His emphasis on dialogue and more importantly colloquium as involving corporate critical self-consciousness; (7) His conviction that the study of religion although crucial is part of the greater whole of humane knowledge; and (8) His insistence that the views of non-Westerners and persons of other religious traditions must be given due seriousness within this greater whole (Whaling, *World's Religious Traditions*, 6). All eight of these concepts have, seemingly, stood the proverbial test of time in the ensuing forty years. They are a testament to Smith's legacy, indeed.

2. Smith, *Meaning and End of Religion*, 25–26.

3. Smith, *Meaning and End of Religion*, 29; 213n45.

Conclusion

a historical tradition which has been institutionalized through a process of reification. Whereas *religio* denoted personal piety, *religion* refers to an abstract entity (or transcendental signifier) which Smith claims does not exist. Smith has argued that while objective empirical evidence and corroboration is necessary for meaningfulness of a religious statement it is not sufficient unless there is confirmation also by the subjective testimony of the insider or member of the respective faith.[4] An integral part of faith, Smith asserts, is a personal response to that proposition or experience. Faith implies engagement and interaction, while belief involves only an intellectual assertion that something may be true and correct.[5]

In his classic study, *The Meaning and End of Religion*, Smith proposed the term *religious tradition* as more adequate than *religion*, for it is a cumulative, dynamic, and historical term connoting movements, not systems. Perhaps it better conveys the reality of religious movements that are more like rivers than monuments— rushing then slowing, converging and splitting, always in motion. To adequately study any religious tradition means looking at its texts and authoritative sources, its interpreters and theologians, its poets and prophets, its activists and reformers, its institution builders and subverters, and all that they have built and subverted.[6] All of this is part of the cumulative religious traditions we have come to call "Christianity" or "Hinduism." For Smith, the study of religion is not so much a set of texts, philosophies, and practices, but the people and communities who have lived their lives and died their deaths in the various worlds of meaning we have come to call *religions*. Not only are the religious lives, texts, icons, and rituals we study situated in particular and inevitably complex historical, intellectual, and cultural contexts, so are we who attempt to understand them. Smith recognized that speaking "about" needed to be replaced by speaking or conversing "with."

In the third volume of his *Systematics*, Tillich more exactly defines and correlates the universal and particular, a universal

4. Smith, *Towards a World Theology*, 60–61.
5. Smith, *Faith and Belief*, 4–5, 50.
6. Eck, "Personal Reflections," 47.

ultimate concern as the basis of the particularity of its culminating expression in Christianity. Here he writes simply, "In this formal sense of faith as ultimate concern, every human being has faith."[7] Then he goes on to describe specific religions as giving to formal faith, thus understood, material content. Against the background of the universal dynamic of the essential as the basis of all religion, Christianity is then singled out as the "fulfillment toward which all forms of faith are driven."[8] The problematic of Christianity as the fulfillment of all religion is a tension that remains in Tillich throughout his career, although I only mention such here because I here focus on the way Tillich works to establish humanity's universal religiosity as the basis of a humanizing economy between the divine and the human, which itself is based on an essentialism as the prior condition to whatever concrete form the essential might assume in existential incarnation. At this point in the discussion it becomes obvious that only against the background of a universal religiosity does Tillich understand any specific religion, including Christianity, to be truly humanizing.[9]

Faith can destroy us or heal us, but according to Tillich we can never be without it. Tillich's definition of faith helps us to perceive the religious element of our lives not simply as one component among others, but as that which unifies all our life's efforts, beliefs, and attitudes. Faith, for Tillich—not belief—is the *only* thing capable of unifying human life among its disparate elements and concerns. But more so, that unifying result is also its definition: faith is simply that state of ultimate concern. Indeed, for Tillich, faith is the state of being ultimately concerned; notably, the content matters infinitely for the life of the believer, but it does not matter for the formal definition of faith.[10] Faith is real in every period of history. This fact does not prove that it is an essential possibility and necessity. It could be—like superstition—an actual distortion of man's true nature. This is what many people who reject faith believe. The

---

7. Tillich, *Life and the Spirit*, 130.

8. Tillich, *Life and the Spirit*, 131.

9. Dourly, *Paul Tillich, Carl Jung*, 30.

10. Tillich, *Dynamics of Faith*, 16.

Conclusion

question raised by this book is whether such belief is based on insight or on misunderstanding, and the answer is unambiguously that the rejection of faith is rooted in a complete misunderstanding of the nature of faith.[11]

Tillich helps us infinitely to see how faith is about the whole nature of our lives. His concepts can give us a proverbial road map to discern how the various elements of our lives and the images of our cultures impact the state of our ultimate concern. Faith is not simply the beliefs that we form (although they are part of how we make sense of our ultimate concern and what it implies for our lives), nor is it simply what we do. Instead, faith is about the orientation of our whole life. And for that lesson, Tillich's definition of faith is worth pondering. Faith is not simply the will to believe, says Tillich; it is a cognitive affirmation of the transcendent nature of ultimate reality. This is achieved, not simply by a process of intellectual inquiry, but by an act of acceptance and surrender.

According to Tillich, religious faith brings an awareness of the sacred. Tillich says that faith is certain, insofar as it is an experience of the sacred, but that it is uncertain, insofar as it brings finite beings into relation with an infinite reality. The element of uncertainty in faith cannot be avoided, and must be accepted. Tillich argues that doubt is included in every act of faith. The dynamic concept of faith helps to explain the interaction between faith and doubt. Every act of faith recognizes that there may be a possibility for doubt. Faith as ultimate concern requires the courage to make a personal commitment. The risk involved in faith is related to the presence of uncertainty. Faith may become nondynamic, or static, when the risk of uncertainty is excluded by a law, creed, or doctrine. Thus, faith may be either: dynamic, when uncertainty is recognized and overcome by faith, or nondynamic, when the possibility of any uncertainty is excluded by faith. Tillich believes that the truth of faith does not conflict with scientific truth, unless faith claims to express scientific truth, or unless science expresses faith in a particular model of reality. The truth of faith is also independent of historical truth, and historical truth is independent of the truth of

11. See Tillich, *Dynamics of Faith*, 115.

Conclusion

faith. Tillich says that the truth of faith can neither be affirmed nor denied by scientific, historical, or philosophical truth. Faith is true insofar as it adequately expresses a concern with ultimate reality.

The dynamics of faith are evident in the conflict between participation in and separation from ultimate reality. Tillich explains that faith by its nature includes separation, for if there is no separation from the object of faith, then it becomes a matter of certainty, and not of faith. Participation in ultimate reality brings certainty to faith, but separation from ultimate reality brings uncertainty to faith. Doubt can be suppressed by conventional, or nondynamic, faith. But nondynamic faith can become dynamic faith. Tillich contends that the triumphant aspect of the dynamics of faith is that faith cannot be rejected or denied, unless another faith attempts to replace it. Thus, faith is necessary and universal. Tillich's broad understanding of faith as ultimate concern provides an interesting and fecund basis for theological discourse unrestricted by a rigid dogmatics.

By Tillich's criteria, it is possible to have true faith, but to have false beliefs at one and the same time. It is also possible to have true beliefs, but false faith. In the more accessible *Courage to Be* lectures, Tillich argues that the only credible form of religious belief is an absolute one where Christianity criticizes its concrete symbols and embraces a God beyond theism.[12] Since religion gives belief-based answers to questions that philosophy poses, it must be the elemental character of the human situation in which the definitive answer to anxiety can be found. So Tillich looks to the individual-or-participant structure of the person's selfhood and finds that in the middle between mystic absorption into the ground and personal encounter with a so-called "divine person" one finds faith.[13] Tillich offers a holistic concept of faith; no element is supreme, but all are included into the synthesis. It also implies an integration of philosophy and theology. Tillich's ontological definition of faith seeks subject-object union, intellectual and emotional integration, and a creative dialogue between theology and philosophy; it is this

12. Tillich, *Courage to Be*, 188–89.
13. Tillich, *Courage to Be*, 156–57.

Conclusion

last implication of faith as ultimate concern which has far-reaching significance for the method of philosophy of religion.

Tillich also contends that faith is both conscious and unconscious. Since faith is the total act of personality, it is impossible to imagine faith without the unconscious elements of one's personality. Faith as a conscious act relies on the unconscious elements to create faith. If simply unconscious forces determine a mental status, Tillich states, it is not faith but rather compulsion. He also states that faith is freedom. "Freedom is nothing more than the possibility of centered personal acts."[14] Since faith is a free and centered act of personality, freedom and faith are equal.

The very title *Dynamics of Faith* leads to the question, What is faith? In answering this rhetorical question, Tillich stipulates that faith can hold many meanings, especially when used in the context of religion. In fact, "Faith is the state of being ultimately concerned: the dynamics of faith are the dynamics of man's ultimate concern."[15] Tillich also states that the concern must be unconditional. For Tillich, faith doesn't have to necessarily be religious; it also can be nonreligious. However, Tillich contends that faith is a centered act: "Faith as ultimate concern is an act of the total personality. It happens in the center of the personal life and includes all its elements."[16] The human mind's most centered act is faith; everything revolves around faith. It is not simply a function or section of a person but his or her total being. Tillich states however that faith is more than the sum of a person's parts or impacts; it can involve rationality and it can involve emotion, but it transcends them both. Faith can have an impact on both rationality and emotion without destroying both in the process, for it is what Tillich calls "ecstatic," which means one can stand outside themselves without ceasing to be themselves.

Tillich, in view of such, speaks of many types of faith. These types vary from religion to religion, culture to culture, and even from individual to individual. The variance in these faiths has to do with the variation of symbols of the faith. These types all have

14. Tillich, *Dynamics of Faith*, 6.
15. Tillich, *Dynamics of Faith*, 1.
16. Tillich, *Dynamics of Faith*, 4.

one thing in common. They all are united because of their focus on "ultimate concern." Faith is the central phenomenon in the personal life of mankind. It is visible and invisible at the same time. It is both religious and nonreligious. It is universal and set in stone. It can be changing but is always the same. Tillich states that it is "an essential possibility of man, and therefore its existence is necessary and universal."[17] If faith is our "ultimate concern" then it cannot be undercut by science, superstition, or distortion of church and state. Faith alone stands upon itself and justifies itself.

In short, for Tillich, faith does not stand opposed to rational or nonrational elements; rather, it *transcends* them in ecstatic passion for ultimate reality—that is, the ultimate concern. According to Tillich, faith is an act of the total personality. Thus, the dynamics of faith must account for the dynamics of personality. As such, faith is the freedom to choose to believe in something. Faith is "ecstatic" in that it is a centered act of the total personality. It should also be noted that Tillich does not exclude atheists in his exposition of faith. Everyone has an ultimate concern, and this concern can be in an act of faith, "even if the act of faith includes the denial of God. Where there is ultimate concern, God can be denied only in the name of God."[18]

I would now like to offer a theological assist to my six interlocutors throughout this book (Wilfred Cantwell Smith, Robert Cummings Neville, Roland Faber, David Ray Griffin, Paul F. Knitter, and Paul Tillich) from none other than Paul Tillich, in part because what he cautions against implicitly is still a reality, and what he suggests still needs to be done. Tillich spells out three forms of religious provincialism which in the context he obviously thinks are still extant in the contemporary theological climate; all of these need to be done away with in order for a proper theology of religions to be asserted. The first is the most all-encompassing. It is simply designated "Christian provincialism" and in context means the denial of the redemptive efficacy of non-Christian religions.[19]

---

17. Tillich, *Dynamics of Faith*, 115.

18. Tillich, *Dynamics of Faith*, 52.

19. Tillich, "Christian and Non-Christian Revelation," 60.

The defeat of this provincialism would recognize the salvific validity of other religions and deny to Christianity its traditional claim to a culminating ultimacy and salvific capacity to which all other religions were ordered and to which they would submit. The defeat of this provincialism would obviously negate the claim of any religion to possess an exclusive or even superior means of redemption than that to be found in another. In effect, at this late date, 1961, Tillich is still fighting the doctrine of *"extra ecclesia nulla salus,"* or "outside of the church no salvation."[20]

The second provincialism is the "provincialism of theistic religions."[21] This provincialism would reduce religion to a relation to a transcendent and, usually personal, divine entity. Here Tillich is combating that form of Christian theological provincialism which would deny the status of religion to communities bonded without such a God. The obvious target is any form of literal biblical theism based exclusively on a relation to a wholly transcendent and personal God.[22] In amplifying this point Tillich endorses as "great religions" the Buddhist, Confucian and Taoist traditions who thrive without the kind of God described by biblical personalism.[23]

The third provincialism is that "provincialism of religion proper over against the powerful quasi-religions of our time."[24] In the light of his identification of the quasi-religions in these lectures, Tillich is here conferring on communism, nationalism, and humanism a certain religious status as expressions of the underlying holy and, in so doing, implicitly affirming their values to be religious and at least potentially redemptive of their members. In amplifying this form of provincialism, Tillich argues that such secular quasi-religions have "points of identity with religions proper."[25] Behind each of them there is always "a background of a religious character in the

20. Dourly, *Paul Tillich, Carl Jung,* 4.

21. Tillich, "Christian and Non-Christian Revelation," 60.

22. Dourly, *Paul Tillich, Carl Jung,* 4–5.

23. Tillich, "Christian and Non-Christian Revelation," 61.

24. Tillich, "Christian and Non-Christian Revelation," 60–61.

25. Tillich, "Christian and Non-Christian Revelation," 61.

proper sense of religion."[26] One cannot escape Tillich's implication that certain forces and the communities they create often identified and dismissed as "secular" by a provincial religious perspective can be themselves the bearers of salvation.[27]

However, in the third volume of his *Systematic Theology*, Tillich belies his aforementioned views on provincialism with his own *lingering* provincialism. Indeed, therein he posits a universal revelation as the generative source of specific revelations that grounds the distinction he draws between "formal faith"—a universal ultimate concern, and "material faith"—the inevitable and diverse expression of formal faith in finitude. In the lingering provincialism just alluded unto, Tillich goes on to describe Christianity as the identity of formal and material faith and so as the culmination of religious history, that is, "the fulfillment toward which all forms of faith are driven."[28] To identify formal and material faith, thus understood, as coalescing in Christianity, was an unfortunate and constraining position in years past.[29] However, armed with insights from Smith, Neville, Faber, Griffin, and Knitter, we may go into the future reality of religious pluralism primed and ready to defeat once-for-all any remnant of Christian provincialism. May we go forward then, and attempt just that.

26. Tillich, "Christian and Non-Christian Revelation," 62.

27. Dourly, *Paul Tillich, Carl Jung*, 5.

28. Tillich, *Life and the Spirit*, 131.

29. Dourly, *Paul Tillich, Carl Jung*, 5–6.

Bibliography

Armstrong, Karen. *The Great Transformation: The Beginning of Our Religious Traditions*. New York: Anchor, 2006.

Baumard, Nicole, et al. "What Changed During the Axial Age: Cognitive Styles or Reward Systems?" *Communicative and Integrative Biology* 8:5 (Sept. 2015) e1046657. https://doi.org/10.1080/19420889.2015.1046657.

Bellah, Robert N., and Hans Joas, eds. *The Axial Age and Its Consequences*. Cambridge: Belknap, 2012.

Bilmoria, Purushottama. "The Meaningful 'End' of God, Faith, and Scripture." In *The Legacy of Wilfred Cantwell Smith*, edited by Ellen Bradshaw Aitken and Arvind Sharma, 49–68. Albany: State University of New York Press, 2017.

Borg, Marcus J. "Jesus and Buddhism: A Christian View." *Buddhist-Christian Studies* 19 (1999) 93–97.

Cox, Harvey. "Faith and Belief Revisited." In *The Legacy of Wilfred Cantwell Smith*, edited by Ellen Bradshaw Aitken and Arvind Sharma, 82–91. Albany: State University of New York Press, 2017.

Dourly, John P. *Paul Tillich, Carl Jung, and the Recovery of Religion*. London: Routledge, 2008.

Dunne, John S. *The Way of All the Earth: Experiments in Truth and Religion*. South Bend, IN: University of Notre Dame Press, 1978.

Eck, Diana L. "Religious Studies—The Academic and Moral Challenge: Personal Reflections on the Legacy of Wilfred Cantwell Smith." In *The Legacy of Wilfred Cantwell Smith*, edited by Ellen Bradshaw Aitken and Arvind Sharma, 44–53. Albany: State University of New York Press, 2017.

Eisenstadt, S. N., ed. *The Origins and Diversity of Axial Age Civilizations*. Albany: State University of New York Press, 1986.

Bibliography

Faber, Roland. *The Becoming of God: Process Theology, Philosophy, and Multireligious Engagement.* Eugene, OR: Cascade, 2017.

———. *The Divine Manifold.* Contemporary Whitehead Studies. Lanham, MD: Lexington, 2014.

———. *The Garden of Reality: Transreligious Relativity in a World of Becoming.* Lanham, MD: Lexington, 2018.

———. *God as Poet of the World: Exploring Process Theologies.* Louisville: Westminster John Knox, 2008.

———. *The Ocean of God: On the Transreligious Future of Religions.* London: Anthem, 2019.

Griffin, David Ray. *Deep Religious Pluralism.* Louisville: Westminster John Knox, 2005.

———. *Founders of Constructive Postmodern Philosophy: Peirce, James, Bergson, Whitehead, and Hartshorne.* SUNY Series in Constructive Postmodern Thought. Albany: State University of New York Press, 1992.

———. *God and Religion in the Postmodern World: Essays in Postmodern Theology.* SUNY Series in Constructive Postmodern Thought. Albany: State University of New York Press, 1989.

———. *God Exists but Gawd Does Not: From Evil to New Atheism to Fine-Tuning.* Claremont, CA: Process Century, 2016.

———. *Primordial Truth and Postmodern Theology.* SUNY Series in Constructive Postmodern Thought. Albany: State University of New York Press, 1989.

———. *Reenchantment Without Supernaturalism: A Process Philosophy of Religion.* Cornell Studies in the Philosophy of Religion. Ithaca, NY: Cornell University Press, 2000.

———. *Religion and Scientific Naturalism: Overcoming the Conflicts.* SUNY Series in Constructive Postmodern Thought. Albany: State University of New York Press, 2000.

———. *Two Great Truths: A New Synthesis of Scientific Naturalism and Christian Faith.* Louisville: Westminster John Knox, 2004.

———. *Unsnarling the World-Knot: Consciousness, Freedom, and the Mind-Body Problem.* Oakland: University of California Press, 1998.

———. *Whitehead's Radically Different Postmodern Philosophy: An Argument for Its Contemporary Relevance.* SUNY Series in Philosophy. Albany: State University of New York Press, 2008.

Heim, S. Mark. *Salvations: Truth and Difference in Religion.* Faith Meets Faith. Maryknoll, NY: Orbis, 1995.

Hick, John. *God and the Universe of Faiths.* London: OneWorld, 1993.

Hick, John, and Paul F. Knitter, eds. *The Myth of Christian Uniqueness: Toward a Pluralistic Theology of Religions.* Maryknoll, NY: Orbis, 1987.

Isaacson, Walter. "Einstein and Faith." *Time,* Apr. 5, 2007. https://content.time.com/time/magazine/article/0,9171,1607298,00.html.

Jaspers, Karl. *The Origin and Goal of History.* New York: Routledge, 2016.

Knitter, Paul F. *Introducing Theologies of Religions.* Maryknoll, NY: Orbis, 2005.

Bibliography

————, ed. *The Myth of Religious Superiority: Multifaith Explorations of Religious Pluralism*. Faith Meets Faith. Maryknoll, NY: Orbis, 2005.

————. *No Other Name? A Critical Survey of Christian Attitudes Toward the World Religions*. American Society of Missiology 7. Maryknoll, NY: Orbis, 1985.

————. *Without Buddha I Could Not Be a Christian*. London: Oneworld Academic, 2009.

Knitter, Paul F., and Roger Haight. *Jesus and Buddha: Friends in Conversation*. Maryknoll, NY: Orbis, 2015.

Lindbeck, George. *The Nature of Doctrine: Religion and Theology in a Postliberal Age*. Philadelphia: Westminster, 1984.

Martin, Bernard. *The Existentialist Theology of Paul Tillich*. New York: Bookman Associates, 1963.

Neville, Robert Cummings. *Behind the Masks of God: An Essay Toward Comparative Theology*. Albany: State University of New York Press, 1991.

————. *Defining Religion: Essays in Philosophy of Religion*. Albany: State University of New York Press, 2018.

————, ed. *The Human Condition*. The Comparative Religious Ideas Project. Albany: State University of New York Press, 2001.

————. *Realism in Religion: A Pragmatist's Perspective*. Albany: State University of New York Press, 2010.

————. *Religion in Late Modernity*. Albany: State University of New York Press, 2002.

————, ed. *Religious Truth*. The Comparative Religious Ideas Project. Albany: State University of New York Press, 2001.

————. *Ritual and Deference: Extending Chinese Philosophy in a Comparative Context*. SUNY Series in Chinese Philosophy and Culture. Albany: State University of New York Press, 2008.

————. *The Tao and the Daimon: Segments of a Religious Inquiry*. Albany: State University of New York Press, 1983.

————, ed. *Ultimate Realities*. The Comparative Religious Ideas Project. Albany: State University of New York Press, 2001.

Peirce, Charles Sanders. "Speculative Grammar." In *The Collected Papers of Charles Sanders Peirce*, edited by Charles Hartshorne and Paul Weiss, 2:34–62. Cambridge: Harvard University Press, 1932.

Race, Alan. *Christians and Religious Pluralism: Patterns in the Christian Theology of Religions*. London: SCM, 1983.

Rahner, Karl. *Foundations of Christian Faith*. New York: Crossroad, 1978.

Schleiermacher, Friedrich. *On Religion: Speeches to Its Cultured Despisers*. Louisville: Westminster/John Knox, 1994.

Schmidt-Leukel, Perry. *Transformation by Integration: How Interfaith Encounter Changes Christianity*. London: SCM, 2009.

Smith, Wilfred Cantwell. *Believing: An Historical Perspective*. Oxford: Oneworld, 1998.

Bibliography

———. *Faith and Belief: The Difference Between Them*. Oxford: Oneworld, 1998.

———. *The Faith of Other Men*. New York: Harper & Row, 1962.

———. *The Meaning and End of Religion*. New York: Mentor, 1964.

———. *Patterns of Faith Around the World*. Oxford: Oneworld, 1962.

———. *Towards a World Theology: Faith and the Comparative History of Religion*. Maryknoll, NY: Orbis, 1984.

Stefon, Matt. "The Axial Age: 5 Fast Facts." *Encyclopaedia Britannica*. https://www.britannica.com/list/the-axial-age-5-fast-facts.

Stenger, Mary Ann. "Faith (and Religion)." In *The Cambridge Companion to Paul Tillich*, edited by Russell Re Manning, 91–104. Cambridge: Cambridge University Press, 2009.

Stewart, Robert B. *Can Only One Religion Be True? Paul Knitter and Harold Netland in Dialogue*. Minneapolis: Fortress, 2013.

Swidler, Leonard, and Paul Mojzes. *The Uniqueness of Jesus: A Dialogue with Paul F. Knitter*. Eugene, OR: Wipf & Stock, 1997.

Taylor, Mark C. *After God*. Chicago: University of Chicago Press, 2007.

Tillich, Paul. "Christian and Non-Christian Revelation." In *The Encounter of Religions and Quasi-Religions* by Paul Tillich, edited by Terence Thomas, 57–79. Lewiston, NY: Mellen, 1990.

———. *The Construction of the History of Religion in Schelling's Positive Philosophy: Its Presuppositions and Principles*. Translated by Victor Nuovo. Lewisburg, PA: Bucknell University Press, 1974.

———. *The Courage to Be*. New Haven, CT: Yale University Press, 1963.

———. *Dynamics of Faith*. New York: Harper Torchbook, 1957.

———. *Existence and the Christ*. Vol. 2 of *Systematic Theology*. Chicago: University of Chicago Press, 1957.

———. *Life and the Spirit, History and the Kingdom of God*. Vol. 3 of *Systematic Theology*. Chicago: University of Chicago Press, 1963.

———. *Reason and Revelation, Being and God*. Vol. 1 of *Systematic Theology*. Chicago: University of Chicago Press, 1966.

———. *Theology of Culture*. London: Oxford University Press, 1964.

———. *What Is Religion?* Translated by James Luther Adams. New York: Harper Torchbook, 1973.

Wallace, Anthony F. C. "Rituals: Sacred and Profane." *Zygon: Journal of Religion and Science* 1:1 (1966) 60–81.

Whaling, Frank, ed. *The World's Religious Traditions: Current Perspectives in Religious Studies; Essays in Honor of Wilfred Cantwell Smith*. Edinburgh: T&T Clark, 1984.

www.ingramcontent.com/pod-product-compliance
Lightning Source LLC
Chambersburg PA
CBHW060414090426
42734CB00011B/2312